# I Fell Into the Money Pit:
# Memoirs of an Unlikely Day Trader

———————————

*Chelsea Cramer*

**BoldTrader Publishing**

Copyright © Chelsea Cramer 2009
All Rights Reserved
No part of this document may be reproduced without written consent from the author.

This book is a work of non-fiction based on the life, experiences, and recollections of the author. In some cases, names of people and places, dates, sequences or the detail of events have been changed to protect the privacy of others.

Published by BoldTrader Publishing
boldtraderpublishing@gmail.com


ISBN 978-0-615-33426-4

Cover designed and created by Jeffrey Holmes,

www.loosepaint.com

# Contents

1. At My Peak: A Day as a Part-Time Day Trader  7
2. Becoming a Dancer  17
3. Discovering New York City  31
4. The Long Long Resume  47
5. Exit Stage Left  69
6. Better Than Shopping  81
7. B-B-B-BET!!!!  105
8. Full-Time Day Trader  117
9. Death By Options  127
10. Bye Bye NYC  137
11. The End of A Good Thing  145
12. Currency: The Heroin of Day Trading  167
13. Welcome to the Money Pit, My Furry Friend!  173
14. Out of Money  185
15. Getting Out of a Rut the Hard Way  197

# Chapter 1

# At My Peak: A Day as a Part-Time Day Trader

Tuesday 6:45 AM the alarm sounds. I spring out of bed, turn on the computer, and wash my face while the PC starts up. Earnings season is here so it will be a busy trading day. Companies are reporting their quarterly earnings so there are bound to be quite a few stocks moving on the news. I have been trading for about a year now and I have my routine down. Last night I prepared my trading platform, adding to my watch list all of the stocks that would be reporting their earnings this morning. Hundreds. While the stock market doesn't open till 9:30, pre-market starts at 8 AM, and electronic trading even sooner. This is when I scan through my list to see which stocks are the biggest percentage gainers and losers. They are the stocks I will trade when the market opens.

While eating a bowl of oatmeal, I make a list of those moving stocks and start my analysis of them. During earnings season there will be about thirty of these a day. I have to find out what their recent daily volume has been, what time they will have their earnings conference call, how much short interest there is in the stock, and if there has been any recent volatility in the stock. I add this information to my list along with the previous day's close price and the price I estimate it will open at today. Then, to establish the final variable in my trading strategy, I calculate the percentage change from previous close to the estimated open price.

List complete, I get dressed, apply my make-up, brush my hair, and bundle up for the cold trip to the office. I grab my hand held ultra mobile PC and turn it on so it can warm up while I head downstairs. I throw my messenger bag over my shoulder as well as the duffel bag containing my tights and dance shoes that I will need for ballet class after work.

Then the big decision. Do I take the subway and run the risk of delays on the way from Central Park West to Times Square, or do I splurge for a cab, eighteen bucks. The cab is faster and allows me to continue watching the stocks that I plan on trading on my computer, but sometimes the wait for a cab at rush hour takes longer than the ride itself. I decide to walk toward the subway

## At My Peak: A Day as a Part-Time Day Trader

and if I happen to see a cab on the way I'll hail it.

Luckily an empty one pulls up. "Broadway and 44th Street. Go through Central Park please, it's faster than staying on Central Park West," I order the driver. I am too busy staring at my computer to enjoy the scenic drive through the park. Although the leaves are off the trees this time of year and there is a scattering of snow on the ground, there are still joggers and bikers getting their morning exercise in and dogs enjoying their walk in Central Park.

The traffic slows as the driver pulls out onto Central Park South and heads down Seventh Avenue toward Times Square. I get the cash ready to hand to him and sling the bags back over my shoulder. Forget the gloves; I need my hands free to use the computer since the quotes are changing every second. The more preparation I can get done before arriving at the office the better.

"Right here is good," I yell at the driver as we approach Times Square. Sometimes I would rather walk a little farther than sit in traffic as my blood pressure rises. I bolt from the cab, through the traffic, past the slow moving crowds of people, through the turnstile of my office building, and into the elevator. I don't even look up to see if my coworkers are in there with me. They have given up waiting for a "hello" from me.

The elevator doors open, I run down the long hall to the office, through the main door, past the friendly receptionist who also knows not to expect a greeting, and to my cubicle. I sit in a room with sixteen other people and they are all wise enough not to breathe a word to me in the morning. *Do they know what I am up to? Do I care?* I turn on my office computer. While it starts up, I make adjustments to my notes based on the quote changes that have occurred between home and the office. I re-do most of the percentages, determine which stocks are the best for trading today, and prepare my office computer/trade station for the opening bell.

It is now 9:15, and the next fifteen minutes are the most crucial. If I overlook even one variable, I could lose thousands of dollars in the first few minutes of trading. If I am correct, I will make between one and two thousand dollars by 9:35 and I will be done trading for the day. Next I grab my cell phone and run into a private room to call my broker. "Are there any shorts available for TEVA? I'll take 1000 of them."

When I get back to my desk the 9:00 morning meeting that never starts at nine has started. That means I will have to trade while pretending to look like I am paying attention but actually trying my best to tune out the chatter around me.

"Does anyone have any issues to discuss today?" Maria probes. I don't even look up.

My computer screen is ready, I am ready. Although there is no opening bell going off in my office, an

## At My Peak: A Day as a Part-Time Day Trader

employment agency, I imagine it when my clock blinks 9:30.

My first trade executes. I short a stock that is opening 9% lower than the previous day's close. The bottom falls out of it immediately after the open. I cover to close the trade and, within a couple of minutes, I have made $2,000--DONE! I take a deep breath; the tightness in my chest lessens. I have proven another one of my strategies and that is a great feeling!

I listen to my phone messages, nothing interesting, and head downstairs to get an iced coffee with extra milk and coffee cake. When I get back my co-workers have sensed that the air around me has calmed and they say hi and smile as if looking for an explanation for my half-crazed demeanor just five minutes ago.. *What must they think?!*

Throughout the rest of the day I intersperse work with analysis of all of the stocks that I could have potentially traded this morning. The one I chose worked out very well but this is no time to rest on my laurels. I need to look at the charts for the other stocks to see if, had I traded them instead, they would have worked. The more times I can replicate the strategies I have developed, the more confident I become in them and the more risk I will be willing to take next time I see the same situation. It has taken a year to get to this point. After stacks and stacks of hand-written stock analyses, I have finally made it. I am now confident that I can do this full time.

For lunch I treat myself to risotto at a fine restaurant in the area. I will work it off tonight in ballet class anyway. Finally five o'clock comes around and I am out the door, coat and hat on, bags slung over the shoulder. My co-workers are still on the phone. Looks like a long evening for them.

I hop on the subway up to Seventy Second Street and make my way to the dance studio. When the elevator door opens on the third floor, there is a sea of bodies in tights stretching on the floor, or standing up, anywhere they can find a space. Groups of dancers huddle around the door of studio B. The previous class is about to end and theirs is about to begin. It feels like a sauna. Thankfully they keep it warm for the dancers who are clad only in tights and leotards.

I sign in and rush to the dressing room to get out of my hot coat and into dance wear. Everyone is in a hurry either to get ready for class or get back into street clothes after a day of dance and go to dinner. I manage to stuff my office clothes into the duffel bag and, fully changed, find a spot at the vanity to put my hair up. Looking more like a ballerina than stock trader now, I head out to the lobby to find a corner to start stretching.

Stretching before class is a monotonous but necessary part of dancing. If I don't spend at least thirty minutes

## At My Peak: A Day as a Part-Time Day Trader

warming up I could snap a hamstring on the first *battement*. I have never been naturally flexible but look it as I split left, right, and center. Some days with more ease than others.

Stretching complete, I gather my bags and wait with the herd of dancers outside of studio C. This is my favorite class. It is attended by those who have a professional career on stage, want a professional career on stage, and a handful who should never be near a stage. *God, I hope I'm not in that category!* I drop my bags in the corner and find a place at the barre for more stretches while we wait for the teacher to start class.

After plies, tendues, rond de jambs, battements, and countless other barre exercises, we are warm, very warm. Nothing turns a studio into a sauna faster than the heat from an old radiator. Sweat soaks my leotard. Some dancers are actually standing in a puddle of sweat by the end of the barre exercises.

Next we move the barres to the side of the room and stand in the center for adagio. This is a slower combination that usually includes leg extensions and turns, and allows for musical interpretation. My leg may not be as high as the freakishly flexible girl in the front or I may just turn twice instead of the dizzying five revolutions that the guy next to me has mastered, but I am holding my own considering that the day is starting to catch up with me. After a series of turning and jumping combinations down the floor, we applaud the teacher and accompanist, grab our bags, and race to the dressing room.

It is now 8 PM and I am ready for dinner. Outside the air is still freezing but after the strenuous ballet class it actually feels good. I take the long walk from Broadway over to Central Park West, stopping at the Chinese restaurant for vegetable noodle soup. *Great, one more thing to carry.* I choose to take the subway up Central Park to my condo. It feels good to sit down and the cars are not that crowded at this hour.

At home, I spin around in the shower for a second just to rinse the sweat off. I will take another shower later when I finish my work. While eating, I begin preparing my trading platform for tomorrow and finish any analysis I was not able to complete at the office. Some nights this continues till midnight. Then I shower and fall into bed.

# Chapter 2

# Becoming a Dancer

I grew up in a small town in upstate New York. My elementary school years were filled with playing Barbies, playing house, school, office, anything make-believe. Middle school was a chance to get to know students from other elementary schools and I became a little more social. When I started high school I also started dance.

When I was thirteen years old, I attended the dress rehearsal the night before my friend's dance recital. I had never been to a dance class or seen a dance recital and didn't really care to. I was busy the night of the main show so she had to settle for my going to the rehearsal. I had my camera ready to snap a few shots of her on stage in her frilly costume.

# I Fell Into the Money Pit: Memoirs of an Unlikely Day Trader

That night was the run-through of the show and very informal. The house lights were on and parents were walking in and out of the auditorium to help their kids backstage. I was not ready for the effect that show would have on me. I had no idea that bodies could turn and jump like that and that feet could tap dance! It's hard to explain the feeling you have when you see something for the first time and know it is what you were meant to do. I used up the whole roll of film before intermission. The teacher came out on stage to make corrections after each class performed and direct them on how to improve and what changes to make. *I WANT TO DO THAT!* Next fall I enrolled.

My mom and I went to the dancewear boutique at the mall and I tried on all of the leotards. I finally settled on one that was mostly gray with a geometric design. In the dressing room I thought I looked great. After purchasing the leotard, jazz shoes and tan tights, I was ready for my first class. I couldn't wait to get there!

The studio was on the second floor of an old historic building in my town. I found my place in front of the mirror along with the other eighteen students. Boy, did I look skinny in my leotard next to them! I was all arms and legs. I looked like a bird. Then the teacher walked out on the floor, and she was also very skinny, whew! I stood next to her. First was jazz class. Learning the steps came quite easily for me. Sure, it was only a beginner class but it was all new. I was a little discouraged in the second half of class, tap. At the end of the session, I approached Miss Sara with my new tap shoes. "I think they're broken. They don't sound like yours, they just make a thudding sound."

"They're just not broken in yet. Once you tap in them for awhile the sounds will become clearer," she explained, but I think she really meant that my feet needed to be broken in.

As the weeks progressed I gained more and more confidence. The teacher used me to demonstrate exercises down the floor, which built my ego. I was quickly learning that I had a "body for dance." Looking like a twig was finally a good thing!

"Are there other classes I could take?" I asked Miss Sara. She invited me to join another beginner class that met on Tuesdays right after school. These kids were younger, maybe eleven or twelve years old. Because most students my age had been dancing for a few years, there weren't many other options for me. I quickly became the best in the class and loved when other students were being scolded for not learning the dances while I was being praised.

At the end of the year when it came close to recital time, Miss Sara had us each dance the routine by ourselves so she could assess who really knew it and who was just following along. I executed the entire dance flawlessly. The other students were stopping in the middle, forgetting steps, and bearing the brunt of Miss Sara's wrath.

"Chelsea, you don't need to pay for class this month. You obviously know the dance and it's not fair to you to have to wait for everyone else to catch up!"

For that compliment, I would have paid double!

I was advanced to a more challenging class in my second year. This group was actually my age. Still, everything seemed very doable. I was becoming more flexible and had discovered that I could turn easily.

I was also fifteen and starting to grow and develop. Yet, I was still having trouble even keeping a training bra in place. Without adequate cleavage the god-awful thing kept creeping up. By lunch time it was practically around my neck! I wanted so much to grow up to be like my dance teacher. Judging by her body, I decided that curves would not be seen as a good thing so I had to stop the process now.

I knew I could do it by controlling my calorie intake. I remember one day when I ran into Miss Sara at a local fair. I was eating a candied apple when she smiled and said "hi." I couldn't even look her in the eye, I was so ashamed that she saw me eating. By the time recital season came around, I was maintaining my 90-pound weight by skipping lunch and, instead of dinner, just eating a small bag of trail mix. I was very impressed with my will power.. *Maybe I really can be a dancer!*

"You are so *skinny*!" My friends exclaimed when they saw me in my costume. I beamed.

The next year I was invited to attend a national dance competition. It would take place in the summer so to prepare I wanted to make sure I had a great tan. I spent one scorching afternoon floating on a raft in my neighbor's pool without a drop of suntan lotion on. I was determined to go from pasty white to glowing tan in one day! That night the pain was unbearable. My skin was bubbling up and my mom spent the whole night covering me with cool washcloths. I was literally in too much pain to move. This is a tradition I would repeat every year. I always overdid my first summer days in the sun.

It was during the summer that I also developed an intensive exercise regimen. In the morning I would go for a long walk followed by a bike ride. Then I would come home and work out on my stepper machine while watching TV. I would have a yogurt for lunch then start practicing dance routines in my mini dance studio in our basement. To cool off, I would follow this with a swim in my neighbors' lap pool.

Too much exercise on too little food does not make for a pleasant disposition. Unfortunately for my mom, I had just turned sixteen, and she had volunteered to teach me how to drive. She had witnessed hair brushes flying out of the bathroom on bad hair days, belts whipping across my bedroom when I couldn't put together the perfect outfit, as well as other memorable teenage moments. Nothing, however, prepared her for the dreaded Bad Driving Day. I can only imagine her fear being in the passenger seat with me at the wheel but, God bless her, she stuck it out.

Very patiently she navigated me around town, to the dance studio, mall, all the essential places that I would need to go on my own. Everything went smoothly until one day when she thought that she told me to take a certain turn, I swore she didn't, and we found ourselves in the wrong place, and wrong lane at the wrong time. "YOU TOLD ME TO TURN HERE, NOT THERE!" I screamed.

"I thought I said turn there...meaning up there," she responded calmly.

"NOW I'M GOING THE WRONG WAY! IT'S YOUR FAULT!"

The car was not as soundproof as I had hoped; heads were turning. By the time I got my license my mother was being treated for severe hypertension. Some coincidence, huh?

High school graduation finally arrived. After being accepted at all three colleges I had applied for, I chose to attend a private college close to home and close to the dance studio so I could continue my involvement there. By this time, I had been moved up to the most advanced dance classes. I compensated for my lack of talent and charisma with practice and more practice. I envied the other dancers who had natural ability or had a "face for the stage." I thought that if I worked hard enough I would be able to dance professionally "someday." There was always time for my "look" to develop. To get my teeth fixed, nose done, hair un-frizzed from a decade of perms, etc, etc, etc..

Wisely, my parents encouraged me to have a back-up plan, not to major in dance in college (as if I was good enough to actually be accepted into a dance program). I thought that since I wanted to become a dance teacher, Elementary Education was a suitable major. In my second year of college I was scheduled to take a curriculum class. The professor was preparing us for student teaching. I nearly had a panic attack. I realized that once I became an elementary school teacher, *teaching* would be my lifelong career! I just couldn't do it. If I started down this path, my dreams of being a dancer would be caput. I needed a vague major so I could get a vague job that I could leave as soon as I became talented! The next day I changed my major to Psychology.

I didn't let myself have the usual college experience. I liked that I had dance classes to get to and classes to teach off campus. I didn't have time to attend the floor meetings in my dorm where girls wore PJ's and ate tubs of ice cream. I didn't go to parties where everyone would drink and drink till someone got alcohol poisoning and had to be rushed to the ER (sadly, a frequent occurrence). Well, I went to one.

"We're going to a house party tonight. Want to come?" Jasmine asked as I passed her in the hallway.

It was Friday night and I had all weekend to get my work done so I decided to see what all the excitement was about. I walked over from the dorm with Jasmine and two other girls. Two of them had money to pay a beer cup at the door; Jasmine and I brought our own sodas.

Upon entering, I wasn't impressed. A room full of not-so-good-looking people trying too hard to look like they were having fun. There was a game of strip-something going on in one room and I really didn't want to see any of them lose! In the living room alcohol was the only topic of conversation.

"How many Jello shots can you do?" Drunk Guy asked.

"I don't know, let's see! *Giggle, giggle,*" Drunker Girl responded.

"I have to pee again but I can't walk up the stairs, I'm too drunk!" Another girl shouted.

After escorting her up the long flight I wandered

around the hallway past the occupied bedrooms. *What is this, a brothel?*

I spent the night playing with the house cat. A very nice stray. There was some sneezing but overall not a bad date.

I certainly wasn't the ideal roommate. I was too busy to socialize and too tired to chat after dance class. My roommate, Tara, was also a dancer but she decided to take a break from it and enjoy college life.

"I brought my pointe shoes with me. Do you want to go down to the lounge to practice?" Tara asked.

A few of us were hanging out in our room and I think she was more interested in showing off than anything else.

"I don't really want to," I responded. I had just started taking pointe and knew that she was much better than I was.

"You can all come and watch me!" She said as she grabbed her dance bag.

We all followed Tara down to the small lounge in the basement. There was a sofa and TV in the corner and the rest of the room was empty. There was indoor/outdoor carpeting on the floor but that didn't stop Tara. With pointe shoes properly tied, she proceeded to execute fast pique turns in a circle. We all oohed and aahed on cue. Then, there was a loud *snap* and Tara was on the floor. Trying to turn in pointe shoes on a rug was a mistake. A tendon in her ankle snapped. After a few minutes it swelled up to twice its size and someone volunteered to take her to the emergency room.

"Someone should go with her," Jasmine said as she looked straight at me. A good roommate would have. I didn't. All I could think about was the mountain of work I needed to get through before the next day.

My time was spent writing papers and tackling the infinite amount of reading before I had to leave to go to the studio. I tried to get a week's worth of reading done in one night but I retained nothing. I was on overload. I could always manage to bang out decent papers on my laptop, a novelty at a time when most students were trying to manage with old fashioned word processors.

Fearing temptation, I didn't keep food in the dorm room. So, when Tara was out, I ate her food. She kept a plastic container full of raisin bran. I would eat cups full dry and, after the level had gone down far enough to be noticeable, I would refill it with the contents of the little boxes they sold in the dining hall. The many hours of practice in the studio and strict dieting paid off when national dance competition time came around that summer. No "freshman fifteen" for me!

## COMPETITION WEEK

**Saturday 5:30 AM** I wake up extra early to get ready and get the last of my belongings packed before my dad calls "all aboard" and he, my mom and myself begin the long drive down to Myrtle Beach, the location for this year's national dance competition. By 7 AM we are all in the van and ready to start the trip south from New York State.

**Day 2** We are winding through the scenic hills and I have turned green with car sickness. I tell my parents to drop me at the nearest hotel and enjoy the rest of the trip without me.

**Day 3** We finally arrive at Myrtle Beach. I must have lost five pounds on this trip so far. One benefit of car sickness. My equilibrium is so off from the drive that everything looks slanted.

**Day 4** We have a free day before the competition starts. Informal practices are held in the parking lot, hotel lobby, wherever we can find space. The hotels have been taken over by dancers. The other guests don't stand a chance. That afternoon we invade the pool. I take a good long look at myself in the mirror before I head down. My even slimmer figure pleases me.

**Day 5** Competition begins. The competition takes place in the evenings, and during the day the dancers take classes from well known teachers and choreographers. I am the only one from the studio that gets there at 9 AM for the very first class. I don't want to miss a thing. I find that it is quite difficult to learn in a large room filled with hundreds of dancers. I envy those who pick up the combinations quickly. I just don't have a knack for that. That night, the dressing room at the theater is packed with dancers and their moms all trying to stake out their territory. The air is thick with hairspray. Aside from the petty bickering among the stage moms, the evening schedule runs smoothly. I am comfortable with the routines and love being on the stage. I don't get nervous at all. I have been sure to only eat salads when we go out to dinner. Some of my spandex costumes are not very forgiving.

**Day 8** Awards are handed out in a grand ceremony. I carry an armful up to the hotel room. My bedroom at home is now filled with trophies from the numerous competitions I have attended through the years.

**Day 9** We head home; this time I have a good supply of Dramamine.

# Chapter 3

# Discovering New York City

What does someone do with a degree in psychology after graduating from college? Grad school! Where does someone go to grad school for psychology if she wants to be a Broadway dancer? New York City!

I am sure there are more affordable ways to get to the Great White Way, as Columbia University doesn't come cheap. Still, not losing hope that I would wake up one day with natural talent for the dance, I packed up my tights, leotards, and dance shoes, and moved to New York City. More specifically, graduate student housing in New York City.

My first residence, however, was the Waldorf Astoria Hotel. Don't get jealous, it was just for a week while I danced in a competition being held there. It was exactly what I expected my life in the city to be: a cushy suite to lounge in by day and a fabulous stage to dance on at night. Performing on the stage set up in the grand ballroom gave me the feeling of having finally made it, however temporary.

That was only for a week. Time for reality. For anyone who has not looked at apartments in Manhattan, allow me to explain. Anything under $1500 a month at that time would not be livable, my rent...$350 per month.

Let me take a step back. Before leaving home I had decided to let go of my obsessive compulsive ways. I didn't follow up with student housing to make sure they'd received my application which I, of course, sent in, complete, the day after I received it. With only a couple of weeks until I was due to move and no housing assignment, I decided to call.

They'd never received my application for housing! I was stuck with the least desirable accommodations, a room the size of a closet with a communal kitchen and communal bathroom/shower in which I often heard a girl "communing" with her boyfriend. In spite of this, I was gung ho about my grad school major. Organizational Psychology sounded so professional and business-like! Maybe I could be an Organizational Psychologist by day and a Broadway dancer by night!

A week later, I started attending classes in Human

## Discovering New York City

Resource Management and Business Theory in the large lecture halls of Columbia. I tried my best to look interested but quickly learned that this had to be the most boring major ever. My goal was just to get through it and get the Master's degree. No need to enjoy it.

My first class was held in an older building on 120$^{th}$ Street. I felt so young when I walked in. I looked young for my age, not to mention that most of the students had returned to get their post grad degrees *after* having been in the working world. I was green.

We were assigned to small groups to prepare a presentation for the class on a topic in business. The other members in my group had the process down. They knew how to create a Power Point show and had enough knowledge from other classes to piece together a presentation without having to do research. I only had to read the note cards they'd prepared while they showed the appropriate slides. That was fine with me. The more time I had to explore the city, the better.

That same week I set out to find a dance studio so I could start taking classes. Unaware of how gawky and clueless I would look in a professional dance class setting, I registered at one of the best studios in the city.

Enthusiasm and desire, however, does not a dancer make. Even though I had been dancing for seven years, I did not realize that dance learned at Miss Sara's School, Anytown, USA, is worlds away technique-wise from that of even the most basic classes I would walk into in New York.

Now, I did not realize I wasn't good right away. No, no. Not even after repeated polite requests by the teachers to "step to the back, please." I came to class early, made sure that I was stretched out enough to split left, right, and center. I could certainly execute a series of turns down the floor or a complex jump combination. But, what these choreographers were teaching was different--all about style, acting, and learning the dances quickly.

I must have looked like a lost duck some days. I couldn't remember what came next and was a beat behind. I constantly found myself going against the flock, so to speak.

A few weeks later I was taking tap class. My teacher started laughing uncontrollably in the middle of a routine. I was working so hard and really thought I looked good.

"You look like Lucy Ricardo when she took dance class," she howled. As someone who loves Lucy, I took it as a compliment. *Note to self: add musical comedy to resume.*

One day around the same time, sweaty from class and somewhat discouraged, I made my usual stop at the deli salad bar and then went down to the Columbus Circle subway station to head home, if you can call it that.

## Discovering New York City

Instead of catching the local train on the upper platform, I went down one flight too many and wound up on the Express. I didn't realize my error until the train started passing all of the stations on the way uptown. Then the train went down, farther underground and faster.

I was scared half to death! Where was it taking me? I'd learned how to get from Columbia University to the dance studio on the Broadway Local and that was it! I knew that if I went far enough I'd end up in The Bronx and I was sure that's where I was going!

I had a plan. I would get off at the next stop and hop in a cab, hopefully before I was mugged for my salad and dance shoes. Do they even have cabs in The Bronx? I could feel the color drain from my face. I was trying to look cool but something about a skinny girl in a little powder blue dress with sweat running down her face did not say "cool."

Finally the train screamed to a halt. I walked up the stairs to the street like I knew exactly where I was going.

NOT A CAB IN SIGHT.

*No skyscrapers, so I can't be in Manhattan!*

People yelled at each other, kids screamed, the sun beat down on the street.

*This must be The Bronx!*

Finally, among what appeared to be a sea of downtrodden, unapproachable people, I found a professional couple wearing suits, holding briefcases, and yes, smiling! Whew! I ran up to them

"Do you know where I can catch a cab around here?"

"Hmm. I don't see any, but good luck," the man responded without stopping. They'd looked at me like I was from another planet.

I turned left onto a narrow street and started to walk even faster and with purpose. I tried to exude confidence.

*Yes, Bronxians, I know where I am going...LEFT.*

I found a cop car parked on a side street. By this time I was almost in tears.

"I live near Columbia University and got on the wrong train. I don't know where I am! Could you pleeease drive me home?"

I practically climbed into the car through the window.

"You live five blocks away, Miss," one cop responded dryly. "You're in Harlem. Just walk that way. Don't go through the park, though, too dangerous. Lots of muggings there."

Not what I wanted to hear. Tears returned.

"We aren't a taxi service. You'll be fine getting there on your own."

Arms swinging, I walked home at an alarming rate, glancing behind me from time to time only to see that they had decided to hang back and follow me to make sure I made it.

## Discovering New York City

Home at last, that little closet apartment never looked so good! Not good enough, though. I missed the Waldorf and the luxury I knew the city had to offer. I set out to find a health club like those you hear about on TV with the rooftop pools, celebrity clientele and, of course, state of the art gym equipment (but that wasn't so important).

After several tours I settled on a top rated health spa on 57$^{th}$ Street. The lobby was beautiful; I felt like I was walking through a freaking mausoleum! After a rocket-propelled elevator ride to the top floor, I entered a beautiful pool area with a sunroof. Sold!

There I spent my afternoons crisping in the sun. My latest diet of Twizzlers was working very well to keep me in top bikini shape. After a day of lounging I graced the dance studio with my presence and then headed off to class at Columbia.

Perhaps you are thinking that I lived off of a very juicy trust fund. The fact is my parents were extremely generous and supportive of my pursuits in the city. But after about six months of easy living I started to feel somewhat guilty. Maybe it was time to call in a favor from one of my college professors and get a j-o-b.

I think my parents' response was "really?!" Honestly, I think they would have been just as happy if I had become a career student.

I got my first job because someone I knew, knew

someone who knew someone else. Actually I had no office skills to speak of, but I could do research. As the word passed down though all of the 'someones,' I soon gained a great reputation as a researcher. I was in.

For three days a week I was paid $18/hr at a well known organization in Manhattan. I was now a businesswoman!

On my first day I decided, since the job was all the way on the east side of Manhattan, I would spring for a cab ($20 each way during rush hour traffic). I waltzed in fifteen minutes late.

My boss was very polite and didn't seem to care. I was shown to my cubicle to drop off my things and then taken on a meet-and-greet tour of the organization. There was a lot of handshaking, polite smiles, and introductions to people who honestly didn't seem interesting enough for me to take the time to remember.

My first task was to assist in the development of a survey that would be used in a brand equity study my boss was heading up. Early into the project I came to the realization that offices are the most boring places in the world! There was nothing remotely interesting in what I was doing and the world would definitely go on without the results of this study. However, I was determined to give my role as a businesswoman a fair shake so I stayed.

Around this time I discovered that New York is filled

with great places to eat and offers a variety of vegetarian foods that I had never experienced before. Something about working in a boring job in a cubicle makes one quite hungry. For the first time since I started dancing I let myself eat ... really eat.

My dance teacher back home had made it clear that if you were serious about dance, you had to be skinny and I *really* wanted to let her know that I was serious. I may not have been the best dancer but I could certainly be one of the skinniest, if that would help.

I'd tried many odd diets including the cooked cabbage diet, saltine with jam diet, dry Shredded Wheat diet and on Sunday when I had my main dance class, I ate nothing, just drank cups and cups of coffee. At my lowest point, I ate only one jelly candy for lunch and drank a lot of iced tea.

My most desperate moment came in the dorm in college. I didn't want to eat but I needed energy to get my papers written so I could get to the studio in time to teach. I grabbed a packet of cocoa mix and ate it, right out of the packet. Not that hot water would have added any calories, I just wanted to get the benefit of the sugar that much faster.

I was able to hide my dieting from family. It wasn't like I was losing weight, I had always been thin. I just wasn't letting myself gain weight as healthy teenagers do.

I didn't understand that my heart palpitations, which lasted for minutes, were a side effect of my extreme dieting. I didn't understand that the white "fuzz" appearing on my body was actually a symptom common to anorexics. I thought I was cursed with having irregular and excruciatingly painful periods, but that also was a result of self-starvation.

However, now that I had become a working woman, I felt I could ease up on my dieting. I was actually being valued for something other than my body type. On the way to work I'd stop off at the deli for a bagel and cream cheese sandwich and chocolate milkshake. For lunch I'd have a bowl of pasta at the casual Italian restaurant near my office.

On my days off, I would go to the deli near Columbia that made awesome veggie burgers and vegetarian burritos; they must have weighed two pounds each. I'd finish them off with a pint of "fat free" coffee-flavored ice cream. (I feel nauseous now just writing about it!)

Talk about diet rebellion! My weight went from 105 pounds to my highest of 128 pounds. When I saw that number on the scale I thought I was going to DIE!

After a few months, I knew I couldn't stay at that snooze of a job anymore. I gave my boss notice and she came back with an offer of full time work with a raise! I politely declined and she was stunned. Hers was a highly respected organization and I don't think anyone had ever turned down an offer to work there.

Now I had some free time. I have always loved dogs. I grew up with a dog my parents adopted before I was born, a stray Lhasa Apso aptly named Stink. That breed can be beautiful with their long hair but, after having lived on the streets, he was one smelly snarl of fur when he was found, they tell me.

From an early age I had always supported dog shelters and various animal organizations, monetarily. I wanted to do more now, though. I really wanted to adopt a dog but living in an apartment and not getting home till 8:30 PM after dance class made that plan unrealistic. I decided to take a walk over to the shelter anyway just to look.

I passed the cat room (too allergic to even go in). The dog room, as I expected, was filled with the resonating barks of over twenty inmates. I found it so hard to walk by each cage--a tile floor with a drain in the middle and no blankets. Some dogs had lost their fight. They just lay there giving me the most sorrowful looks as I passed by. Others barked so hard that all four paws left the floor.

Thank goodness none of the dogs really called to me. No threat of walking out with a new pet. I did, however, find information about their volunteer program. Perfect! I submitted my application for dog walking and a couple days later got a call to attend a new-volunteer training session.

Eight other new volunteers and I met after work in the shelter's board room. The volunteer coordinator led us though the procedures.

First, when we arrived to volunteer, we were to pick out a dog to walk, sign in and make sure that the dog hadn't just come back from a walk. Then we were to leash it. This involved opening the cage door just enough to get to the dog's head to slip it into the leash.

We were warned to hold the door with a firm foot so it wouldn't open too far or else the dog would shoot right out.

I cringed when I found out we had to use choker collars. (I advise anyone thinking of using one of these on a dog to first try it on, pull it taut and see how it feels!) Then the trainer explained that the purpose of these collars was to aid in training. They weren't meant to be cinched around the neck all the time, only when the dog disobeyed and we had to give a fast tug as a correction.

We were also told to carry newspapers, as the law in NYC says to clean up after your pooch. Lastly, we were instructed to grab a handful of treats to use as a reward for good behavior. After the session was over, I was ready to become their #1 dog walker.

That Saturday I put on my bright red volunteer dog walker t-shirt--they'd given one to each of us--and headed over to the shelter. I took a lap around the cages and chose a sweet, foxy looking dog, not too big, lots of fur, cute. No need to take newspaper, I had gone to the pet supply store and purchased handheld poop picker-uppers. I found a leash and collar that would fit the dog and headed for the cage.

Now, they say that animals can sense when someone is hesitant and not acting like the leader in a situation. Fur Ball had me sized up from the get go. I opened the cage and *whoosh*, out he ran into the main room. He was so surprised that he'd actually made the escape that he proceeded to run amok, and so, round and round he went.

Finally a staff member approached.

"Let me help with that," he said calmly.

Obviously Fur Ball knew he was a leader. He sat right down and let the man leash him. That done, I was handed the reins and we headed for the door. I was so flustered at this point that I forgot the all-important treats.

Once outside, Fur Ball was back to running amok. All the other dogs trotting by were heeling and wagging their tails, but not mine! The other dogs seemed to look down their long noses at Fur Ball like he was the obedience school dropout. At least the other volunteers were friendly.

"Awww, he's so cute! You should have a nice walk

with him!"

*Yeah right!*

Finally he slowed down, hunched over and did what he had come out to do...doo. I'm not sure what they fed those dogs, maybe the night before had been Mexican night at the pound, but my little scooper was not going to get the job done. I didn't have newspaper so took a quick look around, saw that we were alone, and bolted, Fur Ball in tow.

The heat was unbearable, the afternoon humid. I'd chosen the hottest day of the summer to take the dog out. After only two minutes into the walk, sweat began dripping down my face. My shirt was soon soaked. The choker collar was not working as intended; unless a dog walks slowly, he'll be constantly choked by the damn thing.

I couldn't take it anymore. We headed back toward the shelter and I was ready for a fight. I couldn't imagine any dog *wanting* to return to its cage, but Fur Ball did. He went right in and sat, obviously waiting for a reward treat, which I'd forgotten to pick up.

"How did it go?" the girl at the desk inquired. She'd just seen us leaving! How did she think it went?

"Fine, it's just very hot today."

I signed out after my five minutes of volunteer duty, went home, and wrote a nice donation check to the shelter. I knew my place.

# Chapter 4

# The Long Long Resume

What in the world do I want to do? I had been in New York City for about six months. My exposure to all of the talent in the Big Apple had dampened my dreams of opening up a dance studio. Even though I had experience teaching dance and I had actually learned a great deal from my classes in the city, I just didn't feel qualified. I knew that there were dancers out there who were so much better than I was. I felt that I needed at least one professional dance experience to prove that I was competent to teach and I was not even close to ready to go to an audition.

I decided to seek an internship in order to test out different career paths. I was called in for interviews with every place that I had applied; artsy companies in The

## I Fell Into the Money Pit: Memoirs of an Unlikely Day Trader

Village, most of the TV networks in New York, and various private companies. I was offered three of the internships and accepted them all: assistant to a talent manager, media relations assistant for a major television network, and production assistant on a national television show. One place that did not call me back...MTV. The internship was casting assistant and they were in the middle of casting for VJs.

"Do you watch MTV?" The casting director asked.

"I am way too busy to watch videos on TV all day!" I responded without even thinking. In any other interview situation that would have been the right answer. Not here. Anyway, three internships at once were definitely enough!

Three days a week I had to be downtown by 7 AM to assist in preparing for the live television show that started at 9 AM. I was amazed how awake and perky the host was at this hour! I strolled in some time after seven on most days barely awake and he already had his makeup on and was greeting the incoming staff. Shouldn't I be greeting him?

My job for the most part was to walk the celebs' dogs, run to get a towel for the flustered hairdresser, make sure the breakfast spread was orderly, etc. One of the guests came with her Pug. That breed is very top heavy, all head and shoulders, no butt. I picked him up and almost dropped him on his ugly Pug snout! *Maybe that's*

# The Long Long Resume

*why that breed has a shmooshed nose!* I apologized and gave him a biscuit.

I was the utmost professional. I didn't ask for autographs from my favorite TV stars when I ran into them in the hallways and I didn't take pictures of them before hair and makeup to sell to the Enquirer (although I'm kind of regretting that one!).

The offices were on the third floor and the sound stage on the second. This show had a unique set that was staged to look like an apartment. When the elevator doors opened, you were basically walking onto the set. I knew I was supposed to be there for the show but I was definitely not hired to be an on air personality. I spent the hour that the show was being broadcast live trying to look like I was staying away from the camera but managing to get on air for a few seconds each day so my parents and friends could say they saw me on TV.

After the show I received the large stack of paper, *The Ratings* for the show that day. All eyes were on me as I took the information that would determine if we would all be there the next day into the copy machine room. There I had to make several copies to hand out at the production meeting that followed the show. The meeting couldn't start till the copies were made and every morning I dreaded doing battle with the ten-foot-long copy machine that was housed in its own room. By the time I found out that the machine could sort, collate and staple a multiple page project, fifteen minutes had passed. Finally I got the hang of it. Flip flip flip went the pages into twenty neat stapled packets. DONE! I removed the stack ready to fly upstairs to the meeting room when I realized that all the pages were blank! Onlookers watched the idiot intern dump all the packets into the trash and start over, this time with the pages right side up.

My favorite task was going to Bed, Bath and Beyond with a fat envelope of cash and instructions on what was needed to decorate the set.

"Chelsea, would you mind going to the store to get a few decorations for the set?"

*Shopping! Finally they recognize my talents!* Two shopping carts in tow, I chose the most outlandish china and accessories: things you would never buy for your own home but which would work just great in a make believe home.

The remaining two days of the week were spent half in the media relations department of my second internship and half in the small quarters the talent management office, my third internship. When I was hired for the media relations department, I was warned that they had no work for me to do.

"We are happy to take you on as an intern but it will be up to you to create your own internship."

## The Long Long Resume

My second day there I found out that he had just quit. I was on my own and no one knew who I was or why I was there. I was left to stroll idly around the department.

"Hi. I'm Chelsea, the new intern. Let me know if there is anything you would like me to help you with today!"

A few people actually looked up from their computer but no one had work for me to do. Although they sure looked busy enough doing whatever it was that they did, no one needed nor wanted me around. I spent the time reading scripts of my favorite TV shows and hanging around the sound stage when the satellite interviews were scheduled. After awhile I realized that this office was no more exciting than any other. TV is supposed to be fun and glamorous but the employees here didn't seem anymore thrilled with their jobs than those at the research organization. When I found myself taking lunch at 10:30 I realized it was time to move on.

Believe it or not, helping the two talent managers in the small cramped office in midtown was the most entertaining. Acting jobs would come in, 8 X 10 pictures would be tossed around till the right pool of actors was in place, phone calls would be made to enthusiastic actors and, hopefully, someone would actually get booked for a job. I was always afraid to answer the phone. Casting directors never introduced themselves, they just started in on what they were looking for.

"We need cute kids for a cereal ad. Seven- to ten-year-olds. Have them at our office tomorrow at ten." *Click..*

"Who was it?" Peter asked.

"He didn't give his name."

(Rolling his eyes.) "What did he sound like?"

"Um, deep voice, heavy breather..."

"Tom. Start calling kids and see who can make it to the call."

Every afternoon auditions were held at our office. It seemed everyone in the city was looking to be represented by a talent manager. Wired mothers would bring in their less enthused kids to read for us.

"Hi...I'm Nancy...This is my daughter Tracy...She's really talented! She looks a lot older than she really is!"

"That's not a good thing in our business," Peter replied dryly.

At the end of Tracy's audition the managers concurred that Tracy didn't have a shot in hell of becoming an actress. Her mom, however, was called back in to read herself.

"Now, she had some spunk!" Peter recognized.

Nervous twenty-somethings hoping to make the jump from school plays to Broadway would find a quiet corner to rehearse lines to themselves before their big shot at a New York audition. Seemingly beautiful men and women filed in only to be put down for having an obvious nose job or boob job. Peter would spin his chair around and mouth to me "bad nose job!" *I can see myself*

## The Long Long Resume

*being a talent manager someday! I'm a Virgo, naturally critical and unaccepting of flaws!*

Although it was all very amusing, Peter, the junior manager, was constantly complaining.

"I need a real job! I have no money! I wish one of these *stupid* actors would book something decent! I can't even afford to live in the city. The train ride out to Long Island is an hour and a half each way. I just sleep here on the couch most nights."

This was a huge red flag. I needed money. No doubt about that. I started thinking that I better start investigating other career paths.

Around this time a light went on. Working in human resources, specifically in hiring, would utilize my major. In a way, it would be like casting. Maybe not so entertaining and fun but definitely more lucrative. I replied to the few ads in the New York Times for recruiters. This is when I learned about the underbelly of the business world, commission paid jobs.

The first office that called me in was a technical recruiting company located in Mid-Town. I was surprised that they actually had an interest in me, since I had no recruiting experience and didn't know a UNIX from a CPU. It didn't seem to matter to the gentleman who interviewed me. I tried not wheeze in his smoke-filled office.

"You'll start in the *pit*." He pointed to a small section of cubicles. "This is where new recruiters spend the whole day cold calling potential candidates. Once you get the hang of it, we'll get you more involved with making actual placements. You can make big money doing that. However, 35K is all we can guarantee for now. By the way, our receptionist is gong on maternity leave on Monday so if you want the job you will have to tell me by tomorrow because I need someone to fill in for her."

I politely thanked him for the interview and left. The nerve of the male chauvinist moron overlooking my Ivy League education and seeing me just as a nice girl who could answer the phones!

A more promising technical recruiting opportunity came through, only there was one catch, it was in Long Island! I was sold on the job immediately when I spoke to Mike over the phone. Boy could he sell! A commute that would involve the subway, Long Island Railroad and a taxi from there to the office, with a base salary of 20K, and for some reason he made it sound like the opportunity of a lifetime!

I hopped on the subway, then the train, then the taxi and finally arrived at their office. The building was a small one-story on a highway with not much else on it. I was just proud of myself for navigating my way around all on my own and getting there on time! I learned that it

## The Long Long Resume

was a family business. The father talked in grandiose generalizations about the bright future of the company and my possible place in it.

"Yep, we are growing fast, real fast! I started this company forty years ago and now I have my son, daughter, and friend working for me. We also have our own receptionist! Soon we'll be listed on the stock exchange. You will of course get shares of the company when that happens."

His son, Mike, told me that I would have my own office and, with a lot of determination, could make upwards of 50K in my first year. His daughter was very sweet and happy to be tucked away in her own office away from the steady stream of BS that was flowing.

*My own office, no smoking, lots of money, SOLD*! On my first day I was introduced to the girl I would be replacing and who would be training me. She looked like she had just come back from war with a serious case of post traumatic stress disorder. She was mumbling, "I just can't take them anymore!" every few minutes while giving me a vague understanding of what she did all day.

The job, according to her, consisted of printing out resumes that had any technical jargon on them from a resume website and jamming them into a fax machine, in html format with the names and phone numbers of the candidates *still on them*, then dialing a client's phone number and hitting send. The next day I came in, she was gone and Mike had determined that I was now a technical recruiting expert.

Finding the resume website, I attempted a few searches, called a few candidates and pretended that I knew what in the heck they did as I flubbed my way through a round of phone interviews.

"Hi, I received your resume. I understand that you are looking for a job as an IT manager. Do you mind if I ask you a few questions about what you do? Actually, could you tell me exactly what an IT manager is?"

Mike seemed content that this was how I was spending my time so I just proceeded until noon when I started wondering where people went to eat in Long Island. The answer? The Roach Coach. I peeked out the window and there it was, a van whose sided opened up like a roach's wings to reveal an assortment of stale food. Yum. I quickly ate my eggplant sandwich (the only vegetarian choice) and decided to go for a walk.

Despite the barren highway that the office was located on, the neighborhood behind it was absolutely beautiful! It was summer so I could walk around the block and admire the mini-mansions that met my expectations of what an affluent Long Island neighborhood should look like. After my "lunch hour" was over, I strolled back into the office to a room of surprised stares. Apparently no one took time off for

## The Long Long Resume

lunch and fresh air was definitely a no-no.

"You're a lightweight," Mike joked.

I had no intention of letting myself become a heavyweight. By the end of the summer I was a zombie. I had failed to see a commission check and had never been so bored in all of my life! I quit.

One good thing about living in abhorable living conditions is that it provides you with an amazing motivation to move onward and upward. Thus I found a call that was even more satisfying that clothes shopping... apartment shopping! Sure, I had no income, but my parents agreed to cosign for me if I found a decent place to live.

I could live anywhere! It would be so cool to say that I lived in The Village! Downtown/Wall Street would put me close to where the money is. Maybe I could even get a job there after I found an apartment! The east side was out. Too far from the dance studio. I pored over the New York Times real estate listings every Sunday, highlighter in hand. I scheduled several appointments with brokers to see apartments in high rises, brownstones, walk-ups, basements, places with a park view, river view, brick wall view, I was open to see anything at the magic price of $1,500 per month.. I could find the positives in any apartment. The brokers loved me, they had no idea where I had been living for the past year.

One appointment was scheduled in the evening and was in a place called Battery Park City. I found it on the map, close to Wall Street, so I decided it couldn't be that bad. I located the stop on the subway map and headed down to see it. I got off at the stop WTC but found, instead of walking out of the subway and up the stairs to go outside, this station led you directly into a MALL. I could live a block from a MALL! I almost cried. I met the broker by the apartment building. The air was still and the breeze smelled like....water! The apartment had a view of the marina on the Hudson River! I tried to control my excitement. The unit was a roomy studio with a separate kitchen, new hardwood floor: *yes, I could definitely tap dance in here!* SOLD!

This is when I learned the difference between shopping for clothes and renting an apartment. No boutique has ever turned me and my money away but, for some reason, the broker gave me the distinct feeling that this might happen here.

"So, where do you work?"

"I'm a student at Columbia."

"So, how are you going to pay the rent?"

"My parents have agreed to cosign for me."

"Well, I'll give your application to my boss and we'll see what happens."

I had the money so did it matter that I didn't have a job and never rented an apartment under my own name before? How dare they ask me where the money was coming from! It was none of their business! I was the customer and I wanted that apartment NOW!

No deal. Later that night I was sobbing on the phone to my mom and dad. I could hardly get the words out. They were probably picturing me lying in traction in the hospital after being run over by a cab.

"I..." *sniff sniff* "....didn't get the..." *snort snort* "....apartment!"

After breathing a sigh of relief they assured me that everything happens for a reason and the right one would soon come along, blah blah blah. After 9/11 one of my distraught co-workers told me that he lived downtown and he couldn't even get into his apartment to retrieve his things afterward. I asked him where he lived. It was the same apartment complex.

As my parents predicted, the right apartment did come along. A professor at Columbia would be in India for two years and I could sublet from her for $950 a month! The apartment happened to be in an a fabulous historic building on Riverside Drive, a very sought-after building on a sought-after street. It was within walking distance to Columbia, another plus. I couldn't believe my eyes when I walked into the lobby. A friendly gentleman, the doorman, greeted me and led me through the marble lobby, which had fresh flowers on the table by the elevator.

# I Fell Into the Money Pit: Memoirs of an Unlikely Day Trader

I made my way up to the $6^{th}$ floor in the small elevator and found the broker. She was the sweetest person that I had met in New York so far. Very grandma-like and without a trace of that wheel-and-deal real estate agent attitude that I had grown accustomed to.

"You are perfect for this apartment!" She chortled.

The unit was bright but old, very old, and small. The studio was square with enough room for a bed and desk. One wall was mirrored so, yes, I could do some dancing there. The bathroom and kitchen looked like they were as old as the building but I didn't care. It had a sunny, cottage feel to it. Plus, it had a sleeping loft, which meant I could have company. I said SOLD and, more importantly, she said SOLD. I now had a Riverside Drive address!

Now that I had a nice new home, it was time to start looking for my next job. This time around, two very different kinds of companies showed interest in me. The first was a well known investment bank downtown. The job was an entry level position in human resources. The other was a large staffing company in Times Square and the job was for an employment coordinator. The first interview was with the investment bank.

Since I had worked in more creative and casual environments over the past year, this was reflected in my wardrobe. I had traded off a more conservative

## The Long Long Resume

trench coat for a black and gold knee-length jacket that was quite stylish at the time. I still blush to think of walking into an investment bank in that jacket. What in the world was I thinking?

Their office was on one of the top floors in the World Trade Center. The interview could not have gone better. I had this process DOWN! Then, I got up to leave, put on my "look at me" jacket and strode out through their lobby, which was filled with a room of international clients in what appeared to be the same blue suit. I saw them look at me, I looked back at the woman who interviewed me and saw that her face had fallen. I couldn't imagine why. The next day I received a phone call from her.

"You are perfect for the position but, I am afraid we will not be making you an offer. You see, we are a very conservative financial company."

I had a feeling she did not care for my sense of style but I honestly did not think it was that bad. After all, I had a blue suit on as well, it was just *underneath* the jacket. It wasn't until a year later when I was cleaning out my closet and gathering clothing for Good Will that I saw that jacket for what it was, ugly as sin!

Keeping this new information in mind, I chose a gray suit for my next interview, paired with a boring ol' trench coat. Could I look any frumpier? Just so happened I was a perfect match with the staffing office, literally. The rug was gray and the walls were gray. I had to get points for that one. Again, a stellar interview. I didn't even get nervous. They made me an offer the next day and I happily accepted.

I thought that working in the staffing field would be just like casting but with a decent salary. It turned out that they were even more critical of candidates than the talent managers were of the actors! The city is a shallow place, not that I was complaining. Taking jabs at someone's outward appearance never loses its fun. I quickly learned the shorthand that the other recruiters wrote on the candidates' resumes. A circle stood for fat, a flower stood for gay, FDA stood for good looking, BOT stood for "back office type" or, in other words, ugly.

Soon after I started the person who had hired me quit. Then another person left, and another, and another. I had just learned their names, darn it! What a waste of time! In my ten years there, the revolving door of employees had become a joke among the handful of us who had the nerve to stick around. There was actually a list that someone kept of all the people who were either fired or who had quit since she had started working there and it went on for pages!

For me it was the perfect job. Not boring, decent raises, and no overtime. An added bonus was that they were located in Times Square, the Theater District. I was actually working on Broadway...kind of. After work I

## The Long Long Resume

could get last minute tickets to Broadway shows at a great discount. My schedule was also more consistent. I was now able to focus more on dance and I was actually looking less and less out of place in class.

When I completed my first year with the company, I also finished grad school and received my Master's degree from Columbia. I used it as leverage to get another raise. My parents came for a visit and we went out to dinner at the revolving restaurant high in the sky in Time Square. I was happy that my life had normalized, and they were looking ahead for me, to my future.

"Now that you have a good income and it looks like you will be staying in the city for awhile, you should start looking for an apartment to buy so you can stop throwing your money away on rent," my mom suggested.

I had never thought about this before, didn't even think it was an option.

"We'll help you with the down payment."

I had seen the coop/condo listings in the paper, units selling for hundreds of thousands of dollars, and I couldn't even conceptualize spending that. They gave me my spending limit: 120K (this could buy a lot back then before the Manhattan real estate market became insane). Apparently they had done some research prior to our discussion. Again I was off on another apartment shopping spree! Yippee!

This time I knew I wanted to stay on the Upper West Side. My parameters were Central Park West to Riverside Drive and 59$^{th}$ Street to 110$^{th}$ Street. Again I was able to visualize the saddest apartments looking like a million bucks after I tried my hand at decorating. I just loved looking at real estate!

I had seen quite a few charming studios and would have been happy with any one of them. I followed up with one more ad before making my decision though. It was for a condo on Central Park West and it was a huge one bedroom, yet still in my price range. I thought it was too good to be true but decided to see it anyway. It was a relatively new building and it had a subway entrance right outside the door. That would mean no more cold walks to the train in the middle of winter when the wind is blowing so hard you can't catch your breath.

I went in a bit skeptical. The condo was just as described, one bedroom with a view of Central Park West and the Empire State building.

"Why is this apartment only 120K?" I asked the real estate agent.

"The building still has part of a tax abatement remaining from 1988 when it was built. It was created with the intention of attracting young professionals to the area. Because of that abatement, there are limitations as far as how much the apartment can be sold for until

### The Long Long Resume

2007 when the abatement ends. Then it can be sold on the open market at any price," she explained.

What a deal! The broker said that I was the ideal buyer for the apartment, given my current salary met their standards. We closed in record time. Mom and Dad helped me paint and clean the rug, which was past being cleaned but acceptable considering I had just acquired a 90K mortgage. I now owned a piece of the city.

## Chapter 5

## Exit Stage Left

*Maybe I should give it a shot just to say that I did*, I thought. I had been at my job for six years and the days were now blending into each other. I needed a change. I bought the trade paper that lists New York auditions and looked for anything that was open to performers who dance. Not dancers who could also sing or act or dance in those little pink torture devices called pointe shoes....just dance.

There were a couple possibilities. I could audition to be a cruise ship dancer, but all of my pay would go towards Dramamine. Plus, I never did care for cruise ships. When I go away on a vacation, I don't want to spend it in an artificial environment. I want to be able to explore the sites indigenous to the land (and by sites I mean the shops and boutiques). *Maybe I could join a dance company!* There was one with an upcoming audition for dancers. Finally, there was one audition for a Broadway show that was still in the development phase.

First, I would need to have head shots taken and make a resume to put on the back of the 8 X10 photos. Since all I had to list under experience was a long list of impressive yet all too common national dance competition awards, I decided to just use a really large font, highlight the height, weight and hair color section, and hope my talent would speak for itself.

Luckily I had just had my braces removed. *Yes, I had braces in my twenties!* Waiting turned out to be a great decision. My problem was unique and, until I moved to the city, I had not found an orthodontist who could correct it without major surgery. My upper teeth were crowded and came to a V instead of a normal U shape. I did not have a toothy grin. I had been told over and over that the only option would be to have my upper jaw broken and the roof of my mouth split and realigned to make it wider. When I was a senior in college, I almost went through with it. I had my wisdom teeth removed, the first step, and my parents gave the orthodontist the non refundable down payment. *Then* I lost my nerve. My mom and dad didn't make me feel bad about it. They knew how difficult that surgery would have been.

### Exit Stage Left

When I moved to New York City, I was determined to find an orthodontist who could correct my teeth with braces alone. I made four appointments and three of the four doctors told me that I was too old, my bones were not malleable enough to be moved by orthodontics only. The fourth doctor put me through a battery of X-rays and concluded that it would be possible. I would have to wear an expander to move my teeth out and braces to shape my smile. On the first night after getting all of the hardware firmly attached in my mouth, I had to learn how to talk again. My *job* was talking and now I sounded like I had a speech impediment! I spent the next week explaining to clients why I sounded drunk. By the second week, I had adjusted and had no problem forming words. I paid through the nose but it was worth it. Over a year later, I had U-shaped teeth!

Now that I had a nice toothy grin, I decided to get it whitened before the big photo session. I wanted the best for my choppers, not the trays, strips, gels, etc. sold in the drug store. I opted for laser teeth whitening at over $1,000 a session. I made my appointment at the midtown tooth whitening spa and headed over after work. My gums still hurt just thinking about it! The procedure itself is painless. You sit in the chair for what seems like an eternity with your mouth open while the blue laser light directed at your teeth does its job. When it is over, they give you an envelope containing your before and after pictures. Wow! What a difference! The next day... PAIN! My already sensitive gums now felt like they contained millions of exposed nerves. Would have been nice if they warned you about this! At least I had white teeth...for about a week.

I had also heard ads for laser hair removal. Wouldn't it be great if I never had to shave my legs again?! An appointment was made with a MD located on the Upper West Side who specialized in this. His office was in a townhouse, small but well-decorated and filled with certificates, which made me feel better. First he slathered cool gel over the skin. Then he tried different settings on the laser to see what level I could tolerate without jumping off the table. Since the bill for this would treatment would dwarf the cost of the teeth whitening session, I wanted to make sure to get my money's worth! I bit my tongue and ignored the pinging laser that felt like thousands of little bee stings. When he was finished, he wiped off the gel and added a thick coat of lotion. *Guess I wouldn't be wearing these pants again!* Within hours my skin turned red and bumpy. At least it wasn't summertime. The next day, no hair! A couple weeks later, @#$&%# HAIR! Rip off.

Grooming complete, I set out to find a photographer who could make me look like the dancer I wanted to be. Out of the hundreds of photographers in the city, I chose the one who could schedule my appointment for the next day, Saturday, since the first audition I wanted to attend was the following week. He had a bare loft on West 14$^{th}$ Street and a terse personality to match.

I arrived on time at 9 AM with no make-up on as he requested. After seeing me I am sure he will never make that request again! He was wearing all black. Black jeans, black button down shirt and black belt. He looked like he was trying really hard to look like a "happening New York Photographer" but it just wasn't happening. We had to wait for the make-up girl to arrive to make me look half way decent before the dreaded picture time.

We waited and waited and waited. He assured me that she was great and couldn't stop raving about her.

"She is a make-up artist but also an actress. She does cartoon voices for Disney!" He mused. "I'm also teaching her how to take pictures. "

Finally, one hour later, she strolled in looking like she just fell out of bed. By this time my adrenaline had worn off and I felt and looked like a tired old corpse. Then the reason for her tardiness arrived, The Boyfriend. Instant tension. Obviously Meek Photographer liked Make-up Girl and didn't appreciate her having just rolled out of bed with Boyfriend and bringing him along. I was hoping for some enthusiasm from Photographer. Some energy, excitement, anything! Zilch. It felt like I was taking a bad high school picture and that is exactly what

I got. Five hundred dollars later I had a box of the worst head shots in the city.

I decided that since my options were slim I would take a stab at the cruise ship audition. Plus, it was scheduled on a Saturday so I wouldn't have to miss work. I got there early, real early. By the time the audition started I had already cooled down after stretching and warming up and was just a ball of nerves in a leotard. I decided I was there for the experience anyway, I could just blend into the masses of dancers. No such luck. Only ten girls showed up! There were more staff and casting directors than auditionees!

"Everyone, come up to the front and make a line," the lady holding the audition ordered.

I didn't want to go up, I wanted to slink out of the studio, but the mob of staff was blocking the door. Obviously their intention was to keep onlookers out but, in the process, they were keeping me in!

"First I want to see each of you execute a double pirouette to the left then to the right."

*Whew, I can do this.* I did a tendue to the side, prepared and whipped around into a clean double turn, then repeated to the left. No cuts were made.

"Now, everyone, go the corner of the room and you will each have a chance to do a tumbling pass down the floor."

That was my cue to grab my belongings and bolt for

the door. I made my way down the ice cold stairwell as fast as I could without bothering to put on my street clothes until I made it outside to safety. First audition DONE.

Next was the Broadway show casting call. Again I arrived early. It was also on a Saturday. It happened to be held at a studio in Times Square only a block from my office so I decided to go there to stretch since they wouldn't let the dancers into the theater until start time. It felt quite odd doing a split in the waiting room of the office. I was hoping they didn't have surveillance cameras! When I felt that I was ready for anything, I headed down to the street.

So much for early. The line of dancers wrapped around the whole block! I can't remember now what my audition number was but I know it had four numbers in it. The line crept slowly. Everyone here seemed to know the drill. They were listening to music and reading books. Many hadn't even put on their tights and leotards.

After three hours, the line snaked inside the theater and my group of about one hundred dancers was next to go into the audition room. During the long wait I had stretched and cooled down at least five times. The combination was a partner dance. Of course, as with most auditions, there were ten women for every one man.

"All men, make a line in the front of the room, please," the choreographer ordered. "Then, women, line up behind a man who is about your height. Make sure there are no more than ten people in each line."

We scurried around trying to get organized as quickly as possible.

"Is this too hard for you to figure out?!" The choreographer sarcastically asked of the whole group. Sure, he had been repeating this same drill for hours now, but come on! Enough with the 'tude!

The men had to perform the combination with each of the women in the line. Great practice but I really felt for the poor guys! They were really sweating by the end. Now, I am not a "partner dancer" to begin with, but trying to learn a combination with a make believe partner and then awkwardly performing it with this sweaty, overworked guy was not easy. I know I looked like a bird dancing with him, long arms and legs and no clue where they were flailing. Only eight dancers in my room of about one hundred made the cut. At least I wasn't doing the walk of shame alone. By the way, that show never made it to opening night.

When I got home, I had the first migraine headache of my life. All I could do was close the blinds, lay on the sofa, close my eyes, and watch the floating squiggly lines. Would all auditions be this bad?

Last but not least, the audition for the dance company.

# Exit Stage Left

This one was happening during the week so I had to take a personal day from work. This time I was ready for the long wait. I had a book to read and didn't even think about stretching till we were inside. I also was proud of myself for dressing appropriately for this type of casting call. No black from head to toe here. No bike shorts or hot pink bra tops either. I wore my suntan tights, Lavender leotard and high heel tap shoes. I did my research and knew what they were looking for.

"Next time I come to audition for them I'm wearing tan tights!" I overheard a girl in blue spandex pants comment. Finally, I did something right!

The first thing they did was measure our height. No need to waste time with someone who doesn't meet the height requirements. I just made the cut off at 5' 6". Definitely a good sign. Then we were divided up and brought into smaller studios with a current company member who would teach us a routine. She walked in and guess what? I knew her! We had taken ballet class together.

"Hi! I'm so glad you came to audition!" She saw me right away. After teaching the group the audition combination, she came over and gave me individual corrections. *How great is this going?!*

Finally the big moment arrived. We were led into the main studio where the directors were sitting at the front of the studio by the mirrors at a folding table with stacks

# I Fell Into the Money Pit: Memoirs of an Unlikely Day Trader

of 8 x 10s in front of them.

"Wait for us to call you out in groups of eight. After you perform the combination, please remain in your place while we make notes. Then, when you are cued, exit to the left side of the studio," the director explained.

I was ready. I knew the combination and, thanks to all of my competition experience, could make a great cheesy smile. The music started and the few counts of eight that we were taught flew by without a hitch. I waited, they gave the cue and I exited. Unfortunately not with the herd traveling left but all on my own to the right! Maybe they didn't notice. Then, I realized, after everyone had had their turn, I would still be over here on the right all by my lonesome! After the next group had their turn, I ran out to join them just as they were being excused and headed left with them. I was cut. At least I still had my day job.

## Chapter 6

## Better Than Shopping

Office work was looking better and better. I went on a few other auditions over the next couple of years but eventually became content to just enjoy the amazing dance classes I was taking in the city. My parents had moved to Florida in 2005, which was fine with me. I would much rather take a slightly longer plane ride to a very sunny place at Christmas than a prop plane to gloomy upstate New York.

I had been visiting my parents in Florida and after a week of eating at waterside restaurants, lounging by the pool, and playing shuffleboard, I felt the wrinkles leaving my forehead. I was actually ready to face New York City again. On my last night before returning, my dad and I were sitting in my parents' living room chatting about my job and general satisfaction with how my life was going at this point.

"How are things at work? Hmm. You have been there about eight years now, right?"

"I really don't mind working there. It is a good nine-to-five job that pays well and I have plenty of time to take dance classes at night."

That's why I was in New York anyway. But how the time had flown by! I knew that dance was what it had always been, a hobby, and that work was what I did not want it to become, a career. My co-workers warned me when I started that I would not be able to work in any other industry. I would be pigeon holed. That was years ago and I didn't care back then. After all, it was just a way to make a living till I became talented! Ten years later, I had no sign of talent and was being referred to as a "lifer" in the office, meaning that I was destined to stay there till I turned gray! Did I really think that the light-colored hairs I had started to notice in my dark brown hair were a sign that I would live the second half of my life as a platinum blond?

"You should investigate the stock market," my dad advised. "Open up a little brokerage account, find a couple of stocks you like and see what happens."

He had been investing since he was in his twenties and had done quite well for himself. Even though my job was not the career I had set out for, I was successful

## Better Than Shopping

at it and the money had been piling up. I had a fat checking account that I took for granted. Money was never an issue. I could walk into any boutique on Madison Ave and buy an outfit, or two, or three without needing to check to see if I could afford it.

Investing had never appealed to me in the past; opening an IRA and 401K was a complete yawn. For some reason though, the idea of "picking out a couple of stocks" had a nice ring to it. It almost sounded like SHOPPING. So, on my last night at my parents' house in Florida, I spent hours at the computer looking at stock symbols. Not knowing a darn thing about the stock market, I was doing just that, looking at the symbols. *Where should I start? With my initials, of course!* Those three letters composed the stock symbol for a small pharmaceutical company. I passed on it. I knew that choosing my two stocks would require a lot more contemplation than that (by the way, my namesake doubled a few weeks after I looked at it, go figure!). Anyway, I settled on two symbols that had a share price of around five dollars. I now had a renewed sense of urgency to get back to NYC.

Usually I had trouble getting up in the morning. The only thing I had to look forward to was the venti frappachino with whipped cream and chocolate sauce that I treated myself to every morning. If waiting in line for it made me fifteen minutes late for work, who cared?

# I Fell Into the Money Pit: Memoirs of an Unlikely Day Trader

No one was going to fire me, I was raking in the dough for that company! However, the first day back from vacation I set my alarm clock a little earlier, got dressed a little faster and skipped the frap. This morning I was depositing a $500 dollar check into my newly opened brokerage account. My eyes popped open when the alarm clock went off and I actually wanted to get up. From that day on, I never had trouble waking up.

The nice men in suits greeted me when I entered the brokerage, which was conveniently only a few blocks from my office. (If you visit Times Square you are sure to see the track that I made between my office and theirs over the next three years.) I had the check in hand and thought I was pretty hot stuff with my big $500 deposit. They treated me like I was.

From there I made a beeline to the office and to my cubicle. I was in a room full of half-cubicles. Sixteen people in clusters of four in a small room where you are only visible to others from the neck up. I was greeted by looks of surprise as I marched in early, minus a tub of frappachino, appearing awake and less grumpy than usual. Of course they had it figured out, I had an...*ahem*....good night, if you know what I mean. They asked what his name was.

The next day the funds I had deposited the day before were ready for trading. The stock market opens at 9:30 and my work day started at 9:00, so that meant I

## Better Than Shopping

had to make my purchase of the two stocks from the computer at my desk. It was a bit bold on my part but I was sure five minutes on the brokerage website wouldn't jeopardize my job. By 9:40 AM the purchases were made. The stocks were sitting in my account, which I had safely logged off of, and my work day had begun. *This should be interesting* I thought. *Maybe five years from now I will go to my account and see that I have doubled my money!* 9:50 AM...*Hmmm, I wonder if I have made any money yet?* I was back on the brokerage site and *OH NO! The price for stock #1 has gone DOWN! I better watch them closely just in case something really bad happens*! By the end of the day they had both crawled down and I was down $150. Still holding the stocks, I decided to wait and see what happened the next day.

 I checked back in the following day at 11:00 and both stocks had crept up to the price they were when I purchased them. *WHEW! Time to sell, this is too stressful!* By 11:35 I was out of those two positions. *Obviously those were not good stocks to have chosen! But wait! My account balance is not at $500, it is at zero! I had better take an early lunch and go see the nice men in suits at the brokerage!*

 In a tizzy I rushed through the door of the brokerage office.

 "I sold the stocks I had but now all my money is gone!" I shouted in the general direction of anyone who was not on the phone.

## I Fell Into the Money Pit: Memoirs of an Unlikely Day Trader

Suit #1 quickly escorted me away from the other customers. This conversation was definitely not good for business!

"After you make a trade, the funds that you used to make the purchase have to settle," he explained. "This takes three days. After the settlement date, that money will be available again for trading."

"What!? I have already chosen the next two stocks that I want to buy and I want in now!"

"If you open a margin account, then you don't have to wait the three days for settlement. The minimum balance for a margin account is two thousand dollars."

Before he had time to take a breath I had my checkbook out.

My trading over the next couple of weeks resulted in a loss of $700, but I had my modus operandi down. Get into a trade, see that it is not going my way and get out at a loss and move on to the next in hopes of making it back.

That weekend I had planned a trip to Miami's South Beach. If I canceled the trip the money I would have saved would have made up for the loss, but I decided to go anyway. As I walked past the trendy boutiques, the $700 was still haunting me. *Think of all the clothes I could have bought with that! I can't believe I just let it evaporate! For some people that is a week's salary and I lost it with a couple mouse clicks! How irresponsible!*

## Better Than Shopping

Instead of shopping I opted to bake on the beach. It was March, and a rather cool day, no need for suntan lotion. After I finally woke up, I decided to take a stroll down the beach. Everyone was looking at me. *I must look mighty hot in my new bikini!* Later that night I took a shower and noticed what all the fuss was about. I was scorched! I have had sunburns before but never so bad that my skin was actually numb. I couldn't feel the burn! I could only see the bright red skin that was developing white bubbles all over. *Gross! I can't look at myself!* I put lotion all over the burn and went to bed.

On the plane ride back from Miami, I realized that long term investing was not for me. Then it came to me. Had I bought the stock as it was moving up and sold it minutes later after I made a small profit, I would have made money without risking those profits by holding it long term. Brilliant!

Monday morning 9:30 AM I was at my office desk with my newly formed plan prepared and mouse poised at the "buy" button.

By Monday 2:00 my brokerage account was frozen and I was issued a violation. *WHAT! I better run down to the brokerage and find out what's going on before I'm arrested!*

Suit #1 greeted me and asked how it had been going. As if the sweat running down my face and my unblinking eyes couldn't indicate my state. Not to mention the fact that my skin was peeling off four layers at a time. This is when I learned that what I had been doing is called "day trading" and that you need a day trading account in order to do this....minimum account balance for this, $25,000.  I had the check written in record time.

Day traders, I have learned, all think they have a system. Does this remind you of something? Substitute Suit #1 for "VIP casino host" and day trader for "whale" and I think you get the picture. Within the next year I had studied the stock market within an inch of its life and made lots of money being in the right place at the right time (when you spend eight hours a day watching stocks move on your office computer you are bound to be at the right place at least once). But, more frequently, I was taking little losses that added up. It didn't matter though. I was honing my craft. I would make it all back after I got the wrinkles ironed out.  I didn't want any discouraging words from my mom and dad. I only told them about the gains and maybe a small loss here and there, but certainly, they thought I was ahead, way ahead.  Meanwhile the nice men in suits saw me often as my balance was frequently dipping below $25,000 thereby initiating a "margin call," which meant a new trip down the street with a newly written check.

I can look back and remember a few moments of

realization when I thought, *Oh my God, I have lost a total of X amount of money! I should just stop now!* One of those instances was the Friday after Thanksgiving. The office was closed on that day but the market was open for half a day so I was able to trade at home. I just couldn't get my act together. Couldn't come out ahead on any trade. At the end of the day I looked at the total gains, or in my case losses, that I had accrued since I started trading and could not believe the number, $47,000! I was numb. I needed air. I put on my jacket and walked over to Riverside Drive from my apartment on Central Park West. I wandered all the way to midtown in a daze. That should have been a turning point, I could have realized that this had gotten out of control and I needed to stop. The voice of reason in the back of my mind was shouting "STOP!"

Recently I had started to listen to a guru of finance give advice on a radio show. I remember her saying, "When you find yourself in a hole, stop digging." I, however, chose to get out the backhoe.

Having no training in the stock market, I was learning as I traded. Had I done some research first instead of jumping in ass first, I would have found out that everything I was trying had been attempted before. I was not the only idiot to try to guess if a stock was going to go up or down on their earnings report. Sure, it's exciting when you enter a whole new world of money making possibilities and notice stocks jump up 40% in one day. You say to yourself, *I missed this one, but the next time this situation comes up, I'll be in on it!* Only to find out that the market doesn't always play out the same way every time.

A few instances stand out. I tried my hand at gambling in the stock market. I bought a thousand shares of a pharmaceutical company the day before the FDA was due to release their decision on a new drug. I was more pumped than a seasoned better at the race track. I did my "research," basically finding every bit of support on the Yahoo message boards that backed up my choice to go long.

After work I walked home, an eighty block trek through a mass of tourists. I had to do something, my nervous energy was building up to a fever pitch. I had the chance to make thousands of dollars in one trade! I was so confident, I called my dad from my cell phone to let him know what I was up to. He could watch as the good news came out and the money started rolling in. He sounded excited for me. Totally supportive. He didn't know how much I stood to lose if I was wrong. I walked at a good clip up Central Park West, my favorite route, fantasizing about how high the stock price was about to go.

I finally arrived home. Sweat was running down my

## Better Than Shopping

face. I took a quick shower while my computer warmed up. The news was due out any minute. I knew it was a lock. The FDA had considered this drug before but told the company that they needed to provide more supporting research before it could be approved. The company said that they had just submitted everything that was asked of them. They wouldn't lie, would they? I researched this same scenario and found the same result every time. When the FDA makes a request for more research and the research is provided, they approve the drug.

7:00 PM: "Approval not granted." The stock price dropped 40% in a matter of seconds. My money evaporated. I called Dad. Still as calm as ever, he simply said, "It happens." How could he be so cool? How did he watch a stock he bought in the 1980's go from $8 to $2 and have the tenacity to hold on to it and finally sell it for $24? Was I really related to him? I took my loss and made a trip to the brokerage office with a new check to deposit into my dry account. *I'll make up for it on the next trade.*

Around the same time I discovered "shorting.." When you *short*, you are essentially starting a trade by selling a stock that you don't own knowing that you will have to buy it sometime in the future, hopefully at a lower price. This is a strategy you would use if you think a stock price will fall. When I first heard about it I thought it was the most wonderful concept in the world. How many times had I bought a stock only to see it turn around and immediately fall right after my *buy* order executed? All stocks that go up must come down!

Unfortunately I learned of this trading tool during the summer of the China solar stock frenzy. China stocks were going gangbusters. Solar stocks were hot. If a company was in China *and* in the solar sector, WHEEEEE. Some companies were gaining upwards of 50% a day for days on end. Of course, after the first day everyone wished they had been on board. The smart ones who recognized this sector trend jumped on in the second day and rode it the rest of the way up. The cautious traders hoped for a pullback before they joined the fun (they never got it). The real idiots thought *Wow, these stocks are up 50% in one day on no real news! They have to go down tomorrow, I'll short them!* Yep, that was me. In some circles I would be called a "bear" or a "contrarian.." Thousands of dollars later, I chose the term "blockhead."

I was sitting at my desk in the office watching my nice diversified selection of shorts ruin me. I decided to hold on, not admit defeat and take my losses. By 3 PM I was having a full out panic attack. I looked around at my co-workers sitting only feet away. They didn't even seem to notice. My face was flushed, my heart was racing, and beads of sweat were running down my face. I was down

## Better Than Shopping

$9,000 and I needed air. I decided to go downstairs to get an iced coffee and think about my next move. Would I hold on overnight or get out by 4 PM? Not having taken the time for lunch, I was past hungry. My mouth was dry. When I returned to my desk, I decided to go to the Yahoo message boards to get some advice. This was always my last ditch source for trading information.

As I sucked down the coffee, I waded through the posts, 90% of which were filled with profanity and name calling without a drop of insight. I was trying to find one knowledgeable trader who could explain what was happening. I found one. He lived in China and explained that the stocks there were soaring in anticipation of the Olympic games. He wrote that his plan was to hold on to his long positions for the whole week, as he was sure the stocks would keep running. It was only Wednesday! I covered my short positions, taking a huge loss. It turned out that he was correct and, had I immediately *bought* shares of the same companies and kept them till Friday, I would have come out even. I didn't have the nerve.

My checking account was getting low. I needed more money to fund my brokerage account. I had heard about home equity loans before and thought it may be worth looking into. I stopped by my bank during lunch. I did'nt tell them I needed a loan to fund my new day trading habit. Thought that may discourage them. I simply said that I wanted to remodel my kitchen and bathroom.

"How much do you earn?"

"108K."

"What do you owe on your current mortgage?"

"70K."

"Do you have any credit card debt?"

"No."

They arranged for an appraiser to come to my home to determine its market value. Since that tax abatement had ended, it could now be sold on the open market. I had no idea what it was worth.

A couple of days later I returned to the bank to see if I qualified for a loan. The banker's eyes popped out of his head when he saw the appraisal. It valued my little condo at 500K!

"Not only do you qualify for a home equity loan, you have enough money in the line to buy a second home if you want to!" I floated out of the bank on a cloud of money.

My mom and dad were very enthusiastic about the real estate investment potential in Florida. They had moved there a year ago and saw many other baby boomers doing the same. Now, keep in mind, they thought I was a born stock trader thanks to my rosy updates and carefully chosen omissions. They wisely suggested that I use my newfound wealth to buy a villa in Florida and rent it out to seasonal tenants. Since the Florida real estate market had just suffered a major decline, this was an opportune time to buy. It just so happened that I had 400K burning a hole in my pocket.

I let my mom and dad shop for me. They toured many homes and emailed pictures and floor plans to me in New York. Finally I got the excited phone call.

"We found your new house! It's perfect, fully furnished, turnkey, and a great location!"

I made an offer that afternoon and closed soon after. I now had a second home. I contacted a couple from the Midwest who wanted to winter in Florida and had taken out an ad in the Florida paper listing their requirements. After a lengthy telephone conversation, I had sold them on staying in my villa. I now had tenants. They were a very sweet retired couple and agreed to pay me in advance for their six-month stay that winter. Perfect. The money from the tenants would cover the expenses of the house. I was set.

After learning what didn't work in trading, I finally found a few things that did. Through a carefully programmed set of trade alerts, I received a pop up message whenever an alert condition had been met. This allowed me to actually get some work done at my place of employment instead of staring at a list of stocks all day waiting for one of them to do something exciting. My favorite alerts were news related. If news breaks while the market is open and you happen to be there the second it does, it is money in the bank. I spent most of my work days glued to my chair. I ordered lunch in, or, if I was chasing a stock all day, sometimes I would skip lunch altogether. One afternoon after a particularly rough morning, I had my first taste of "scalping." This is a trading method by which trades are opened and closed within a short period of time. It was 2 PM and my balance was down to 15K. That meant, unless there was a miracle, I would be making a trip to the brokerage office with a 10K check to bring my balance back up to the 25K minimum required.

Then, my miracle happened. A popup message notified me that ENCY was now a step closer to approval for one of its drugs. My heart started beating out of my chest. I had been practicing in my mind what I would do if this situation occurred and I was ready for action. I entered ENCY into my order entry screen and opened a quote screen that would give me the real time ENCY price. I was in luck! The stock was just starting to react to the news, I didn't miss a thing! I quickly placed an order to buy 2000 shares. Within a minute, the price ran up two points! That was a profit of $4,000! The momentum started to wain so I decided to sell. There

## Better Than Shopping

were no short shares available for this stock so I would only be able to trade it on the long side. As I predicted, the stock gave back some of its gains after the first sprint. I didn't blink for two minutes. I was staring intently at my screen, frozen, waiting for the next entry point. What were my coworkers sitting around me thinking? They knew there was no resume in our database *that* interesting!

Finally the price fall slowed. Those who wanted to take early profits had gotten out. This was the perfect re-entry point. I bought 2000 shares again. My timing was impeccable! I was one with the stock! Up it went, this time exceeding the previous high. I repeated this process again and again until my balance returned to 25K. DONE! Sure, I had just broke even after a long string of losses, but who cared? This was the most exciting twenty minutes of my life!

Of course, chasing news can also have its risks. In a similar situation, I was in the right place at the right time when a news story broke. This time it was bad news. A company had announced at 1:00 PM that they were revising their earnings estimates downward. I immediately put in my order to short 2000 shares. Unfortunately, I had forgotten to set a limit price. I didn't think it was necessary, the stock had high liquidity.

No sooner did I hit the "send" button, than the stock was halted! My order didn't have a chance to execute.

# I Fell Into the Money Pit: Memoirs of an Unlikely Day Trader

Halting a stock is not necessary upon release of important news, but occasionally it will happen. It allows the market maker to assess the situation and set an acceptable price in light of the news. In this case, the price was around $16 just before it was halted. My intention was to sell short and ride it down as the news spread.

Once the stock was halted, I was not able to modify my order. I was at the office and quickly ran into a conference room to call the brokerage but didn't get through in time. When the stock reopened, I would be stuck selling short at the market price, I would have no control. Moments later, the stock did reopen....at $8!!!! My order executed, I had sold short at $8. The price was so unbelievably low that seconds later it shot up to $12. In that short time, I was out $8,000! I finally reached the brokerage; they felt for me but had no recourse. I did not specify a limit price. It was a legal trade. The market maker screwed me and any other suckers who also had sell orders in without a set limit. I had to chalk it up to another learning experience. I just sat at my desk staring at my screen shaking my head. One oversight cost me eight grand!

I needed to find other opportunities to trade. Waiting for news to break throughout the trading day was tedious and, as I had just learned, dangerous. I liked the idea of "scalping," making fast trades when you are only holding on to positions for minutes at a time. That strategy suited me well. I had been a "Headhunter" for eight years, now I had graduated to "Scalper.". I did notice that stocks that open higher or lower than the previous day's close due to news that broke while the market was closed. These stocks had big price swings in the first half hour of trading. Now, I just had to make some sense out of them. Was there a way to predict when a swing would happen and which way it would go? Sure, I could just chase a stock that appears to be heading up or short one going down, but how would I know how long to stay on for the ride? It seemed much too risky.

Some traders really take a hard look at the earnings report and devise their trading plan based on that. I have learned that it's a fool's game. To look at a report that appears to be glowing and then notice that the pre-market trading price for the stock is not that much higher than the previous close, one may conclude that it the price should shoot up at the open. Not necessarily. The fool trader is thinking that even though buyers are not seeing the value in stock now, they will in ten minutes when the opening bell sounds. Idiots! There are so many variables that affect a stock's movement at the open that this strategy is way too simplistic. Months later, when I finally devised a trading strategy that actually worked, I didn't even have to *read* the earnings.

## I Fell Into the Money Pit: Memoirs of an Unlikely Day Trader

My first successful planned scalping trade was of a stock that opened 20% higher than the previous day's close. I had seen this scenario before. I knew it would run up right at the open. Although my instinct was that shareholders would want to take their profits at the open when they saw the huge price increase, I had learned that instincts and feelings can't predict what will happen.

I placed an order to buy 1000 shares of this $5 stock at the open. I had my order entry screen ready to sell those shares seconds after the open. My buy order executed at 9:30 at $5.25. My goal was to make $1000 on this trade so I placed a limit order to sell my 1000 shares at $6.25. A few seconds later the stock ran up as predicted and my sell order executed. The stock went even higher but I was happy with my grand for the day.

A couple days later, I saw the same situation and planned to do the same thing. This was too easy! At the open my trade executed but the stock headed south fast. I lost $1000 as quickly as I had made it before. After the anger wore off, I decided to spend the weekend trying to figure out what made stocks react differently in what appeared to be an identical situation.

I soon discovered the reason for my error the day before; I was treating a high volume stock like a low volume stock. Some stocks may trade millions of shares a day, others thousands. *Of course! This is why my plan*

## Better Than Shopping

*failed!* I now had my second strategy: If a stock opens much higher than it closed the day before AND it is a high volume stock, it will drop at the open.

After months of chart analyses, I finally devised a set of 83 strategies that proved successful over and over! I was actually making money! Up to $2,000 a day, and I was just trading between 9:30 and 10:00 every morning! The "rules," as I called them, were complex. Not only was volume a variable but also the price of the stock, the percent it had changed from the previous close to the open, the exchange it trades on, and more.

I was finally able to enjoy my day without having to sit at the computer waiting for a trading opportunity. I could actually *just* do office work without trying to trade and carry on phone conversations simultaneously. I could even take my lunch hour and get some fresh air.

I loved taking walks around the vicinity of Times Square. To get away from all of the tourists, I would walk west to the more residential, tree-lined streets. Very quiet around noon time. I would peruse the little cafes and restaurants until I made a lunch selection. The maitre d's all knew me. I had "my table" at many restaurants and "my usual" meal.

After having been a vegetarian since the age of fourteen, I decided to loosen up and add seafood to my list of acceptable foods. My body really wanted seafood.

## I Fell Into the Money Pit: Memoirs of an Unlikely Day Trader

Steamed clams, fried fish, shrimp cocktails, were all possibilities now. I was exercising vigorously so it was not affecting my weight. I was at the dance studio five times a week and, when I didn't take class right after work, I would walk home. I enjoyed the eighty-block walk. Sometimes I stayed on Broadway if I wanted to do more "people watching" or, if I needed a quiet walk, I would go up Central Park West. In the winter months, I went swimming at the pool in the UN. Beautiful view of the East Side and East River! A one-day guest pass runs about $35 and you have access to the pool, sauna, and weight room. Not too many people knew about it so many nights I had the pool to myself. My new lifestyle was suiting me just fine!

## Chapter 7

## B-B-B-BET!!!!

Remember that episode of the Flintstones where Fred develops a gambling addiction and whenever he saw a chance to gamble he stuttered "B-B-B-BET!" After watching that episode when I was about ten, I felt a new camaraderie with ol' Fred. Even at that age I knew I was born to gamble. Sure, the stakes were a lot smaller then, a few quarters at the arcade, Necco wafflers at a friendly game of Blackjack, pennies at Auction Day held by my Great Aunt Sylvia (that one will take some explaining). If I didn't have my mom and dad to pull me away, I would still be standing at the Ski Ball machine today racking up prize tickets.

I remember the expression on the face of the arcade attendant when I handed him streams and streams of prize tickets and said I wanted every single "fun pack" in the case. A fun pack is an orange drawstring "mystery bag" full of junk toys that you could get with prize tickets. I had just finished a ski ball winning streak and was ready to cash in before my mom decided that enough was enough. My heart was racing, what a thrill!

I already had almost everything else in the case; a menagerie of stuffed animals, a box full of disposable toys, and a lint shaver (the grand prize, and I still have it). Now I was ready to clean them out of their newest addition, the Fun Pack! I had enough tickets for twenty! The attendant counted them out and held them up to show everyone who had gathered around as I beamed. I was only ten and already the arcade whale! They should have comped me a slice of pizza at the food court!

As I became older and wiser, I learned to stay away from the Lotto counter at the corner store. When I took trips to Atlantic City I never gambled, just watched. I knew if I started I wouldn't be able to stop. I never experimented with drugs and I never drank. I knew I had an addict inside me.

When I was young, my parents never tried to scare me away from alcohol. They also did not tell me that I wasn't allowed to try alcohol till I was an adult. I would have seen that as a challenge. Around the age of eight, if my dad saw me eying his glass of wine, he let me take a sip. I took a careful gulp of the red wine and my lips

## B-B-B-BET!!!!

puckered.

On another occasion I tried a sip of peppermint schnapps. Not so bad but a little strong. The foam was the best part of the beer sip. The beer itself, not so good. I just dipped my finger in the vile-smelling golden liquid known as whiskey. One lick and I shuddered right down to my toenails! Who in their right mind would drink a whole glass of this putrid drink?! It was worse than when I tried to rinse my mouth with my grandpa's Listerine, and that was pretty bad!

Addiction, I believe, is only part of the story. Even when I was young, I had a drive to control any potentially profitable situation. Way back when, my Great Aunt Sylvia would come to family gatherings with bags of knickknacks that she had accumulated over the years and was ready to pass on to the next generation. Being the creative person that she is, she didn't just pass them out, but instead held an auction at the dining room table after dinner was over and the plates were cleared. I don't think anyone took this event more seriously than I did.

Everyone else seemed so relaxed. Perfect! Nothing better than competing with a roomful of sleepy people with full tummies! I had my strategy: I wouldn't use my stack of pennies to bid on miscellaneous household items; I would save them for the end, the time when the big ticket items appeared. Then, when everyone else had just a few pennies left, I would dominate the bidding for the best items! I know it wasn't fair. Those heirlooms were meant to be distributed equally throughout the family. *Tough luck, suckers! Better luck at Thanksgiving!*

In my senior year of high school, I participated in the fund raising event, magazine sales. Of course, raising money for your class is well and good, but this event came with prizes for the top sellers every week! Dad's employees at his office were my target. The poor suckers had no choice. Thanks to them I won a school mug, school blanket, sweatshirts, and stationery. Oh, and I earned a lot of money for my class.

This competitive drive served me well at work at the employment agency. Nothing is more cutthroat than commission-driven work. Yes, I was doing a good deed. I was helping people get jobs! I even received thank you notes from grateful people who had been unemployed for an eternity and finally found their place in the working world thanks to me. After awhile, though, I became less of a do-gooder and more of a lean mean commission-making machine. I went after the most marketable candidates like a vulture. If I was sending someone on an interview and they were scheduled for other interviews through my colleagues, I told my client to make a job offer IN the interview and to even have them start work THAT DAY. I had to get them off the market.

## B-B-B-BET!!!!

I had a good poker face. I let my co-workers do all the yelling when they found out what I had done. I sat there as cool as a cucumber and didn't say a word as I was called every name in the book. Let them make fools out of themselves. I had the strategy, they didn't. In the end, I would have the higher billing, I would make more money, I would still be sitting here and they would be cleaning out their desks. Yes, that job suited me just fine.

In my attempts to avoid the trap of addiction I had been fairly successful. The stock market, however, crept in under the radar. Camouflaged by words like "investing" and "growth" and "retirement planning," I didn't even recognize it for what it really is, THE BEST GAMBLING EXPERINCE IN THE WORLD!

When did I realize that I had an out-of-control stock trading habit? I guess in the first week. I heard the voice of reason in the back of my mind all along the way, screaming, *I can't believe I have lost $700! I need to stop*! A year later....47K, *ugh! I need to ask for help!* Two years later....*I have credit card debt! STOPPP!* I couldn't.

No one who knew (all the nice suits at the brokerage) could help me. It wasn't their job. It wouldn't have been ethical. I didn't want to ask for help from anyone. I didn't want to stop. I could hardly bear the weekends when the market was closed. The adrenaline would wear off and I would crash.

I needed to find something else to do during off hours

to keep me going. I was still dancing and taking ballet classes religiously. Similar to any athletic sport, ballet actually can produce a "high." I was as addicted to it as I was to trading, but I still needed more to get through the weekend.

For years I had made do with the most antiquated computer and dial-up Internet connection out there. I had never liked the computer and didn't like sitting still for fear of getting fat. (I had nothing to worry about. Nothing keeps you trimmer than a good gambling addiction.) I was a dancer, not a computer geek. I didn't even have cable in my apartment. I could get all the information I needed from the five basic channels that my rabbit ears picked up. I didn't want to spend my time on the couch when I lived in the greatest city in the world!

Now, however, I had a reason to upgrade. I needed a fast Internet connection and cable so I could watch CNBC for breaking, market-moving news. I headed to the electronics store and was overwhelmed by the choices offered. I went there every day for a week until I had sapped the salesmen of all of their knowledge and was ready to make my decision. Not only did I pick the best laptop out there at the time, I also got it hooked up and running, all on my own! Sure, I was inside all weekend but I got the job done. I signed up for cable and

## B-B-B-BET!!!!

the fastest Internet connection available.

*Maybe I should wait till I recover my losses before I buy all of this*, I thought, but quickly resolved that there was no way I was going to do my best work on that slow, cream-colored dinosaur of a computer. The nice salesman also showed me the latest in portable technology, the UMPC. This mini-computer has a five-inch screen and is handheld. "Perfect for checking quotes when you are out of the office." He had me sized up.

"SOLD!"

Thousands of dollars later, I was ready to trade on the most current technology out there. Now I could surf the web and do my stock research much quicker. I visited market sites, message boards, every trading resource available. I also fell upon a poker playing site. *This may be fun! I like poker!* I was a bit nervous about playing at an online table with other real people. What if I didn't know when to take my turn? I learned quickly. The site was very user friendly. I only played with "fun money"; that was enough of a thrill. After a couple weeks I had accumulated over a million dollars of completely useless fun money! *Oh well, it is entertaining.*

One Saturday morning I turned on the computer and opened the poker site. I thought I would get a few games in before ballet class. *Whoa! What's this? A jackpot worth hundreds of thousands of real dollars?!* The site had a new promotion. If you played at a real money table, you would be eligible to win a giant progressive jackpot if you got a "bad beat" hand. Meaning, if you got, say, quad kings (a pretty awesome poker hand), and you were beat by an opponent who had a royal flush (a more awesome hand), you would have suffered a "bad beat" and you would WIN THE JACKPOT! In record time I had my credit card out and was making my first real money deposit.

My hands were sweaty as I played my first real hand. I was so worried about losing my money that my strategies went out the window. I only played hands I was sure to win and there weren't many of those. I lost all of my money. I decided I would play at the lowest stakes table and only play $20 a day. If I lost it I was done for the day. I always lost it. I was only playing hands that were potential "jackpot hands." I wasn't there to make money playing poker. I was there to give myself a chance to win the mother lode. I quickly became what they called a "donk" in poker chat.

I was a good client at that site. One day I received a call from a lovely lady with an Australian accent. She introduced herself as my VIP host. *Oh God! I am now an online poker whale too*! She quickly got to the point of her phone call....she was giving me money. She told me I could have twenty dollars on the house at their sister site, an online casino. I could use it to try out their many slot machines. I was never into slots. No strategy there, you are at the mercy of the reels. However, since she was letting me play with house money, I decided to give it a go.

I perused the casino and wasn't too impressed until I saw that they too had progressive jackpots. Only those babies paid out big time! One of them was up to four million dollars! You just had to be lucky enough to hit the right combination. I had found my game! I positioned the mouse on the "spin" button and clicked again and again. My eyes were riveted on the spinning reels. I had a few wins, and my balance was growing! Still, it was small potatoes. I was there for the big mamoo! I clicked and clicked till my balance ran down to zero. Good thing it was house money.

Saturday, 8 AM. My eyes popped open at an unusually early hour for the weekend. I can normally sleep till ten. I had to see if the jackpot had been won! I started up my laptop (AKA the All Mighty Money Burner) and opened up the casino. *It's still there! No one has won it yet!* I quickly made a credit card deposit and started clicking.

Even though I hadn't won the jackpot, I was getting good play out of the game. It took me awhile to lose my money there. After a couple of hours, I was less interested in watching the spinning reels, instead thinking, *just let me know if I win you stupid game!* I set it to auto play with a condition to stop if I had a win over

$1,000 and I went about my day.

After running a few errands I came back to the apartment and it was silent. The casino sounds that the site generates while you play had stopped. *Must be I lost all my money.* I checked the screen and almost fell over. I didn't hit the jackpot combination but did hit something that paid $3,800! Had I found the way to recover the money I lost in the stock market? Was an online casino the answer? For once I made a wise financial decision and withdrew the money. Close to four grand is nothing to sneeze at, after all. A short while later the slots casino closed its doors to US players. Something tells me it was a good thing.

# Chapter 8

# Full-Time Day Trader

I hit my limit. I had been working for the same company for ten years and had become discouraged. I knew I was dependent on the success of someone else's business. Anyone can sit at a desk at a company and fulfill another person's vision, I needed to find out if I could make a living on my own. I didn't want to leave my job till I had recovered all of my losses but, at the rate I had been making money recently, I knew that my trading strategies were working well enough to allow me to take the big step. I had to approach the conversation with the CEO of my company, Mr. Thomas, thoughtfully. I couldn't give him any indication that I had turned my cubicle into an annex of the New York Stock Exchange.

At the end of the day I proceeded to Mr. T's office for a scheduled meeting. Although the agency itself is fairly informal and cramped, his office was spacious with coffee table, sofa, and two chairs at one end and his large desk at the other. Mr. T was always in a suit and always the consummate professional. He welcomed me into his office, expecting to have a typical meeting to discuss my thoughts on business in general. I had been under his employ for so long that I was sure that he, like everyone else, thought I was a "lifer."

My mouth was dry. I didn't want to even start the conversation with him but I had already made up my mind. "I think I have mentioned before that I have been thinking about getting into investing." *Yes, investing sounds a lot better than compulsive day trading,* I thought. "I have been working out some strategies and I think I want to give it a go, take some time off of work, unpaid of course, and see if I have what it takes to trade in the stock market."

I didn't want to come right out and say "I quit." I wanted to leave the door open. That way, if after a couple of weeks I fell flat on my face I could go back.

I think his response was "Hmmm, uh, well...ok." I had to wonder if he knew what I had been doing at my desk. I was paid on commission so I didn't really feel guilty for trading on company time. He was paying me for what I produced regardless of the time it took to do it. I could do my job in my sleep! All the telephone conversations with clients sounded the same. I found it easy to talk and trade at the same time.

It had crossed my mind that maybe he could monitor what employees were doing on their computers. I could imagine him tuning in every morning for the Chelsea Trading Show. *Watch as Chelsea gambles away her life savings before her first cup of coffee!* Maybe he was keeping me around for sheer entertainment! Maybe he was selling tickets at the door! Regardless, he seemed truly shocked by my announcement. In true Mr. T fashion, he was most accommodating. He agreed to keep me on the company benefits during my "leave" and we set a date when I would check in to let him know if I would be coming back. I floated out of the office. I had finally done it!

Back in the cubicle room everyone was attached to their phones trying to wrap up business by the end of the day. One by one I made my way around to most of them to tell them of my plans. Did I forget to say goodbye to a few people? Yes. Did I give fake phone numbers to a few who wanted to keep in contact with me? Yes. I just wanted out. I cheerfully filled three trash baskets with old papers, calendars, shoes, lotion, and everything else that had accumulated in my desk over the past ten years. I took home one bag of personal items but most hit the trash. The girl who sat next to me was more than happy to take a few pairs of my almost new office shoes. I wouldn't be needing those frumpy things anymore!

I gave everyone the same spiel I given told Mr. T, that I would be taking a leave to pursue investing. I wonder how much they knew? Did the people around me with a clear shot of my computer monitor watch me trade? Did they see the huge losses? Did they see me make $1,500 that morning? With my one bag of personal items in hand, I put on my best "I will miss you" face as I ran out of there like a bat out of Hell.

I walked into my quiet apartment with bag in hand and reality sank in. *Oh my God! Did I make the right choice?* At least I kept the window open to return in two months or else I probably would have had a full blown panic attack. I unpacked the bag of junk that really had no other function than to sit on an office desk. Then I had to tell my mom and dad. I opted for the cheerful "Guess what I did today?" approach, quickly followed with "I can always go back in two months if it doesn't work out" and "I still have my medical benefits." I think their response was very similar to Mr. T's. Even though they only knew of the gains I had from trading, not the monumental losses that I conveniently left out, a change like this was bound to lead to hours of nervous conversation between them after we hung up.

No time to think about that, I had to prepare for the

## Full-Time Day Trader

next day, my first day as a full-time day trader. *God help me!* What was I worried about? It should actually be easier not having to worry about the commute and trying to trade with the din of conversation in the office, right? Nothing had changed, I still had my trading strategies and if I stuck to them I should be able to make between one and two thousand dollars a day!

I know people were day traders before the Internet age, but I can't imagine how they did it. The trading platforms that online brokerages make available to their clients are amazing! I had two screens on my desk at home. The laptop screen was where I put the chart for the NASDAQ and Dow markets and a small window containing the official US clock (just to make sure I didn't lose track of time). The wide screen monitor was for the main trading platform. From there I could watch real time charts of the stocks I was trading, make instant trades from my order entry bar, keep track of the news feeds, monitor the bid/ask quotes for as many stocks as I wanted, watch my gains and losses for the positions I had, and study the status of my open orders.

With all of these tools, how was it possible to fail? The charts even blinked red or green depending on the strength of the upward or downward momentum. Any six-year-old who has played video games should have been able to master it!

## FIRST DAYS AS A FULL TIME TRADER

Thursday 7:00 AM the alarm goes off. My eyes pop open and my heartbeat rises to an alarming rate. I turn on the computer and wash my face while the PC starts up. As usual, I eat my oatmeal while making a list of stocks that are moving. This calms me. Routine is good. I skip getting dressed, putting on make-up and brushing my hair. I will take care of that after trading. Right now I want to spend every minute making sure that I am prepared for the opening bell.

9:30 AM *ding ding ding ding*. I can actually hear the opening bell now. I have the TV on and tuned into CNBC. My heartbeat is off the charts. I have my first trade ready, I buy a stock that is opening a lot higher on good news. According to my fail-proof strategies, it will run up right at the open. I will *scalp* it, jump right on for a fast trade and a fast profit.

Open price $22.20. I am in. $21.95....21.70.....21.55. I am frozen, can't feel a thing except for the shooting pain that's going through my chest. I quickly scan the stock variables to see if I missed something. No. What do I do now? Take a loss and re-evaluate later or grit my teeth and hold on? Of course I am stubborn and hold on and, in my first morning as a full time day trader, I have a loss of $2000.

I try to find opportunities to make it back but I am

just treading water. Time to call it a day, get dressed, go down to the coffee shop and regroup before figuring out what in the world interfered with my fool-proof strategy. While drinking my large iced coffee, I replay what just happened. I look for anything that makes this stock and this situation different. Why did it perform in the complete opposite from what I had predicted?

Back at home I am picking up the apartment. The TV is still tuned to CNBC only now I am actually listening to it. I hear the commentators say that the market had sold off right at the open. Not just a small sell off but one that was steep enough to impact the stock I was trading, regardless of how good its own news was. Something to do with the financial stocks. Little did I know what the next year was about to bring!

The next day is smoother, and I make a profit. I enjoy the walk to the coffee shop and smile at the girl working at the cash register as if to say No *need to fear. I know I looked homicidal yesterday but I really am a nice person.* The shop is filled with students and other casually dressed people, a much better group than the rush hour crowd. I sit down at a little table to enjoy my first little victory.

It is a pleasant Spring day so I decide to take a walk through Central Park. I know that I have to keep myself occupied. If I sit at my computer all day I will be tempted to start trading and I am determined to quit while I'm ahead. The park is quiet. I walk along the northern part over to the east side and head down Fifth Ave all the way to Central Park South and back up Central Park West and home. Next I attend dance class and, right after, do my grocery shopping, managing to get home while it is still light out. *This new routine is going to work out very well!*

A few weeks later, I call Mr. T and let him know that I will not be returning. I have relaxed into my new schedule and the stock market has been behaving itself. I am back to making $2,000 a day. All my work is paying off in spades and, at this rate, I will be able to repay my home equity loan in no time! There is no doubt about it. I do not need to work a nine-to-five job anymore!

# Chapter 9

# Death By Options

Options. The word can make the most experienced trader shudder. I had glanced at the options trading page on my brokerage website previously but it looked way too intimidating to attempt. However, many people had suggested that I consider trading options. Satanists! Some investors use options as a way to protect their stock positions. Others buy options contracts because they can bring very high returns with a smaller investment and predetermined loss if they are wrong. Both are legitimate strategies. In the wrong hands, however, options are a surefire way to make your money evaporate!

After about a month of trading fulltime at home, I reconsidered options. I decided just to observe options trading for awhile before jumping in. Google would be reporting its earnings after the market closed on Thursday night so I tracked the options on my watch list. That evening, Google's May earnings report surprised the market. They had a record-breaking quarter. I am still kicking myself for that one! Had I made a $1,000 investment in calls, I would have made a 100K profit! Had I made a $10,000 investment, I would have been a freaking millionaire! Ugh! I'm mad all over again just writing about it! Of course, I repeated the same old mantra, *I'll be there next time.* And inevitably, not since then has there been an options move so great, and I wound up losing a lot of money hoping that there would be.

Here is the catch with options. The contracts you buy expire every month. Therefore, if you take a gamble that a stock price will go up to $15 and you buy a $15 call option for that stock and, on expiration day the stock only hits $14.50, then YOU LOSE ALL YOUR MONEY. Say the next day the stock does hit $15. TOO BAD, YOUR CONTRACTS HAVE EXPIRED! Therefore, not only do you have to know what a stock is going to do but also *when* it is going to do it.

In a déjà vu moment, I noticed that stock options move throughout the day with the stock. So guess what? You can day trade them! *Yes, that is a much better strategy for me!* Why not just trade the stock, you ask? Because the options move much more dramatically so you can MAKE MORE MONEY...FAST.

On my first day trading options, I chose to trade the contracts of a stock that was moving because of news, thereby fitting into one of my regular strategies. Where I would have made around $1,000 on a stock trade, I made $4,000 in a ten-minute time span trading its options contracts instead! *At this rate I will make 20K a week, 80K a month and recover from all of my losses in no time!*

My dad was on a golf trip in Myrtle Beach. Normally I would send him my daily email with $4,000 in large type with lots of exclamation points but I knew he wouldn't have access to his computer so I called his cell phone to relay my success on my first day of options trading. "I knew I could find a way to make over $2,000 a day! I didn't even stay in the trade that long! I could have made even more!" Too bad this would be a onetime celebration.

Of course, anything that can make you money quickly can take it away just as fast, if not faster. On my first day I happened to have had perfect timing. I entered the trade at just the right spot. The next day...not so much. So how did I react? The same way I did when I was wrong about a stock trade, price average. In other words, as the price went down, I just kept buying more. It has to go up sometime, right? $7,000 later I learned, not necessarily!

Had I been trading stocks, the loss would not have been as dramatic. The experienced options traders know that the farther the stock price gets from the options expiration price, the less chance there is of it getting back to that price by the all important expiration day, so the price of the contracts drops faster and faster. Thus, even though I was just day trading options, I still found myself in the same cycle of losing money.

I needed to keep trying. I needed to get back that feeling of making $4,000 in minutes! I just had an off day, I tried to convince myself. If I was able to replicate what I did on the first day, I could even make $10,000 if I timed it right! I just had to study what happened, why it went wrong, and devise a new strategy for the next day.

Attempt after attempt failed. I quickly learned how little liquidity there is in the options market and how easy it is to find yourself on the wrong side of a trade with no way out. I had wiped out all of the gains I had accumulated over the past two months. I already had used up the remainder of the home equity loan. I had to sell my condo. That would be the only way to get out of the hole. I would go back to trading stocks and forget about options altogether.

To tide me over until the condo sold, I took advantage of a "balance transfer" deal that my credit card offered. I had never carried a balance on my credit cards. My credit rating was flawless. Now I needed that money. I had 35K of available credit on one card and the bank offered me an introductory rate of 1.99% APR for one year. Another card offered a 15K credit line, also at a low introductory rate. Anticipating that my condo would be sold within a year, I wasn't worried about what would happen after I lost my low interest rate. I would have them paid off by that time.

Luckily for me, the housing market was at its peak in New York City. The condo I had purchased for 120K was now worth 500K! I would have to pay back the first mortgage, home equity loan and the credit cards, but that would leave me with 130K and NO DEBT. I could start over. I would no longer have the need to take those huge trading risks in hopes of recovering my losses to pay my debts. I could finally breathe.

It was time to call Mom and Dad. "Guess what I've decided to do?" By this time, they must have been afraid to hear my voice on the phone. They did not know of my life-changing losses in the world of options, just that I hadn't had a repeat of the $4,000 day. I had to tell them my rationale for selling my home in the city. I was telling the truth when I said "the real estate market is at its peak! There is no way my little apartment will go for more than 500K and I have a feeling the housing market will drop here soon just as it has in other parts of the US. Now is the time to sell!"

My plan was to stay in my Florida house since the tenants were out for the summer and, after I had been there awhile, decide if I wanted to stay in Florida full time or move back to the city in the Fall.

I quickly scheduled appointments with four real estate brokers who had already sold apartments in my building. Broker #1 started off by saying that he would work for a lower commission: red flag, he must suck. Broker #2 was late for two out of two appointments: OUT. Broker #3 told me that she didn't have much hope that she could sell my condo for the price I was hoping for and that I would also have to hire a "stager" to set up my apartment for open houses and his tab would run in the thousands: GOOD BYE. Broker #4 was a welcome ray of hope. Full of positive energy.

"Your apartment is beautiful! You don't have to change a thing!"

HIRED.

Totally relieved, I cleaned every corner of every room, bought new towels to hang in the bathroom, potpourri to set on the table that I moved to cover the crack in the floor. By the third open house I had the "staging" thing down. I could have that place transformed from lived-in to picture perfect in under five minutes. While the showings were going on, I took long walks around the city. I wanted to see everything that there was to see so when the time came to leave, I would be ready for a change of scenery.

I hadn't been going to dance class as often as I had when I was working, and I really did not miss it. Awhile back I had really done some damage to my knee in ballet. It had been an especially humid day and the marley floor (similar to linoleum and used on the floors in ballet studios) had become almost sticky from the moisture. We had just started the adagio combination and, in the first turn, my body went part of the way around but my foot was firmly stuck in place and didn't move. My knee twisted and buckled, and I was in blinding pain. I was hobbling around for a couple weeks but nothing broke and nothing snapped. Still, even after healing, my knee would often give out when I landed a jump. At this point in my life, I decided that I did not want to risk a serious knee injury and, quite frankly, needed a break from the routine of ballet class.

A month after putting my apartment on the market, I finally got the call. "You have an offer!"

I was right that the housing market in the city was starting a downward trend. There hadn't been any bites on my apartment for weeks and I had been getting nervous. I was so relieved to get the call, I didn't even care if it was a lowball offer. The broker had listed it at 519K and the offer was for 500K. She recommended going back to the buyer with a firm 510K, she did and he bit! Now we just needed to get through the paperwork

## I Fell Into the Money Pit: Memoirs of an Unlikely Day Trader

and closing and I would be debt free.

Chapter 10

Bye Bye NYC

The closing was scheduled for Tuesday and the movers would pick everything up on Monday so my plan was to stay at a hotel Monday and Tuesday night and take a Wednesday flight to Florida. Once there, I would stay with my parents until the movers arrived and I settled into my new home. I was excited. I have always loved Florida and wanted to live there since I was young. I am not a cold weather person and, no matter how much there is to do in New York, once the deep freeze comes you are stuck doing it inside.

Even after donating eight large garbage bags filled with clothes to the thrift store, I still had an enormous amount of packing to do. I underestimated the amount of crap that I had accumulated over the years and had to have the moving company deliver a second order of boxes. I was able to sell quite a bit of furniture on Ebay and I gave the rest to the condo maintenance workers who divvied up the TV, microwave, and chairs among themselves. By 3 PM the apartment was empty. I filled the holes in the walls with toothpaste. Had to make everything look good before the buyer came for the walk-through. There was no leeway for issues.

Finally I was in the cab on the way to the hotel. The moment I had been waiting for. All the work was done! I wasn't the least bit sad when I closed the apartment door for the last time. I was ready to leave the city. With a relieved smile on my face I signed in at the front desk of the hotel on 57th Street and settled into my room. *I just love staying at hotels! I love the smell, the room service, yes, especially the room service!* I ordered linguine and ate while organizing the documents that I would need to bring to the closing.

Around 6 PM the buyer and the broker were going up to the apartment for the walk-through. This is the buyer's last chance to report anything in the apartment that isn't working or is not up to par and make last demands before the closing. Broker and I were holding our breath. Being the queen of take-out, I had never used the dishwasher that was now almost twenty years old. I tried it myself a few days prior. When I flipped the lever it just growled so I quickly shut it off. The next day I called my lawyer and asked that she please put "as is" next to dishwasher in the contract.

For some reason, the buyer made a beeline for the dishwasher as soon as he entered the apartment. Broker called me right after the walk-through and relayed the whole story in her thick Spanish accent. She didn't want a delay in the closing anymore than I did. She wanted her commission check ASAP.

"I held my breath, said a prayer and flipped the lever and guess what? It actually worked, ha ha! The water came in, it swished around, and then it emptied! No leaks! God answered my prayer!"

By her enthusiasm you would think that she had just witnessed someone coming back from the dead! She had to control herself in front of the buyer. "Of course it works!" The next day at the closing she elbowed me and whispered, "I can't believe it actually worked!"

Tuesday morning I woke up early to attempt at least one trade from my hotel room. All I had was my little handheld computer, not ideal if you need to have several windows and a trading platform open all at the same time. I had to try, though. After about five minutes I could see that I was getting nowhere. I decided to pack it in and call it a day.

The closing wasn't until 2 PM. I went on one last shopping trip in the city, had lunch, and went back to the hotel room to get ready. It was a nice Spring day so I walked from the hotel to the office where the closing was taking place. I wore my new white jacket purchased just hours before at Macy's. I had the documents in hand that my attorney asked I bring organized and labeled with Post-its. I couldn't stop smiling.

We all congregated in the boardroom with piles of closing documents. The seller has it easy. The buyer is the one who has to sign his life away. He was in a sweat. After over an hour, the piles of paper were starting to look more organized. We were in the home stretch. The attorneys agreed on the numbers and, more importantly, I agreed with the numbers. (I don't think my attorney appreciated my sitting there with my calculator double checking his work.) Finally I saw what I had been waiting for: THE CHECKS! Sure, a large portion of the proceeds were used to pay off the mortgage and home equity loan, but I still had over six figures coming to me. That would keep my brokerage account in margin for awhile.

The closing wrapped up. We all shook hands and I flew to the bank to deposit my checks. I am a fast walker normally, but I think I passed a few taxis that day. The young teller at the window almost fainted when she saw the size of the check I was depositing. She called her manager over and they informed me that I would not have access to the funds till the checks cleared. No problem, I could wait a few more days.

## Bye Bye NYC

Wednesday morning I took a car service from the hotel to JFK airport. I had been flying since I was a few months old. Flying had never phased me until a trip about a year ago. All it takes is one engine malfunction to ruin the constitution of the most experienced traveler. Now I dreaded leaving the ground. That would be another great thing about living in Florida. I would be living in *the* vacation destination. I would never have to fly again!

On my second day in Florida, the checks cleared. I paid off my credit card balances. I was officially DEBT FREE! A few years ago I would have never imagined myself in debt, ever! Anyway, that dark chapter of my life was over. I had money again.

It took a solid week to get settled in my new house. Luckily, every piece of crap from my apartment fit in perfectly with the new crap that came with the house. I loved my new home! It did feel strange living alone in a house after living for the past ten years on the fourteenth floor of a highly secured condo. I made sure all of the windows and doors were locked. Slept with the phone next to me and kept a screwdriver in my nightstand. I was ready to defend my castle.

The time had come to start trading from my new trade station, the guest room. I sold the bed and set up shop. If I didn't succeed as a day trader now, it certainly wasn't because of lack of technology. I had my desk set up with computer, multiple screens, and TV, which was now essential, given the minute-by-minute changes in the financial sector. I had high hopes that my luck would change now that I had moved.

It was the summer of 2008. I didn't mind the heat in Florida at all, I loved it! My new schedule was ideal. My alarm would ring at 7 AM, I would prepare my trading platform for the morning session, make a quick grand (trading stocks and staying away from options) and have the rest of the day to go out to lunch and shopping followed by a swim in the pool. *This is the life!* Every day I was hauling more and more home furnishings into my new house. New sofa bed, art, decorations, I bought everything. I could afford it now.

At the country club pool, I would relay stories of my trading escapades that morning to eager listeners. I did not look like a typical stock trader and they were very amused listening to me ramble off technical jargon, and they wanted "in" on how I did it. How did I work only a half hour a day and make so much money? I vaguely outlined how I developed my trading strategies but after a couple minutes their eyes glazed over and we all went back to swimming.

# Chapter 11

# The End of A Good Thing

A few months earlier, I had not been at all hesitant to quit my job. I was confident that I had adequately developed my trading skills. As long as I stuck to my "Rules of Trading," I was safe. I could make $500 with hardly any thought at all, $1,000 a day during off season, and $2,000 a day during earnings season. I had a setback with options but that was over. I knew how to trade stocks and that's what I would do.

No sooner had I moved than the whole climate of the stock market changed. It was somewhat gradual to those who had their eyes glued on their trading platforms. First, a few companies in the financial companies were obliterated but the market as a whole was still intact. I decided to play it safe. I didn't try to chase the stocks of those volatile financial companies or try to predict what would happen to them in the long term. I stayed clear of them and stuck to my trading rules. Then September came and WHOOSH.

I didn't lose money the way most people did. I didn't have my life savings tied up in the stock market only to wake up one morning and find out that it had been cut in half. I got into trouble thinking that my style of trading could stay the same despite what was going on all around me. I tried to trade in a bubble. Forget that the market was tanking. I was determined to stay with my trading strategies.

Day by day I was failing. A stock that may have previously been a perfect fit with "rule #21" was now doing the opposite of the strategy that I had carefully outlined in that rule. Stocks, regardless of the sector, were now moving in tandem with the market. I had no way to predict what the whole *market* would do! I had no choice but to just try to jump on something that was moving and hope for the best.

My thought processes were shot. I got into the most trouble by thinking. There was no way to apply rational to what was happening. I tried. If a stock was down 15% by noon, I thought it would have to change direction and tried to find the bottom only to learn that timing a bottom, or a top for that matter, is a fool's game. I just couldn't short a stock that was down so much. It has to bounce off the bottom soon, right?

My losses were adding up quickly. I even started trading options again. I had to make up for all of my mistakes and I needed to do it quickly. Options were the only way. It ruined me. On bad days I was losing 5-20K per day. I was numb. It was time to tell my tenants who were planning on returning to my Villa in the Fall that I would be staying. I couldn't possibly afford to buy a second home now.

I needed money again. I still had my credit cards and, with new offers teasing me in the mail every day, I decided to use them. I maxed out one, again with a balance transfer offer of 1.99% APR that would be in effect for a year. After a few more weeks, I did the same with the other card. Finally, the credit card offers stopped coming. I had reached my limit. It didn't matter. I would figure this market out and make all the money back.

Weeks later I realized that it was harder than I thought. I was having successful days but would wipe out all of my gains with one bad streak. Where else could I get money?

*Maybe I should get a job.* I was now living in retirement central. Most retirees don't need to work; they want to work to be busy. Who do you think companies will hire: someone with less experience who wants a competitive salary, or someone with a lifetime of experience who will volunteer their services.....just so long as they can feel needed? I was screwed. All I could do was try to adapt my trading strategies to fit this new market.

### End of a Good Thing

## A DAY IN FLORIDA

7:30 the alarm goes off. I hear the mourning doves outside my window. I just love that sound! I love waking up in Florida! Despite being deep in the money pit, I still manage to sleep very well. I turn on the computer and wash my face while the PC warms up. While eating my oatmeal I look over the stocks that are possibilities for trading this morning. The man who mows my lawn has arrived and is making circles around my house. I envy him. I want his job. No stress there.

8:30 I try to remain calm as I do my best to find "safe" stocks to trade. I am already feeling nervous. I now dread the opening bell. I prepare my trading platform and write out my plan, back-up plan, and hope-I-never-need-to-use plan. If I actually do something right, I will be done by 10:00 this morning. If I make a mistake, I can use my second plan to recover by 11:00, I hope. If the shit hits the fan, I will be sitting at this @#&%*%$ money burner for God knows how long just grabbing for straws.

9:30 that infernal bell ringing starts. I try to find my first entry point. I now have Rule #19 narrowed down to three possibilities: the stock will go up, down, or not move. This I am now sure of.

9:35 the stock has been bouncing around for five minutes now and I am getting motion sick. I finally just decide to go for it. Long is as good a plan as any. I buy 1000 shares. After getting bounced out of $500 I decide to abandon Plan #1, as quickly as possible.

10:00 I try to find a stock on my watch list that is at its highest or lowest point for the morning session. 10AM is the perfect time for a turning point. I find one, make a decent trade and, by the grace of God, break even! Great day!

10:30 I call Mom to make plans for lunch. She probably can't understand why I am so happy to just have broken even. I am still not telling my parents about those disastrous losses. I have dug myself in so deep that I think the shock now would be too much for them. I'll just have to find a way to make it back.

12:00 PM it's lunch with Mom. I try not to come across like a half-crazed gambling addict who has lost her life savings in a very long losing streak. I am frightened by how easily I can pull off this act now.

1:00 PM I am shopping with Mom. I wonder if she notices that I can now walk out of a department store with no bags in hand? Is she suspicious that maybe my trading hasn't been going as well as I let on?

3:00 PM I take a swim at the pool. I try to gloss over the day's trading events when probed by my neighbors. I wish I hadn't told them I was a day trader!

4:00 PM it's safe to go home. The market is closed and I can no longer make spontaneous, stupid trades. I take

## End of a Good Thing

the evening to review what happened that morning and what I could have done differently. I update Rule #19 adding "stock may do all of the above in the first ten minutes of trading."

7:00 PM I take a long walk around the block. The Florida air smells so clean! I enjoy the view of the beautiful golf courses. *I wish I could just hit a golf ball off the damn tee!*

8:00 PM I log onto the poker website and say a prayer. The jackpot is pretty big now.

10:00 PM having lost all of my poker money, I take a shower and fall into bed. I love falling asleep in Florida!

As long as I had two dimes to rub together, I decided that I would have to keep trying. The money in the stock market was still just "there for the taking." I saw it every day in the charts, just *after* the fact. *If I had bought the GS calls at 9:35 and sold them at 9:45, I would have made $500.* Why didn't I see it when it was happening? *If I had jumped on the GS trade even a minute after the exact turning point, I still would have made money! Ugh!*

I had become afraid of fast turns. I didn't think a trend would last more than a couple minutes. As a result, I became obsessed with getting in at the exact top or the exact bottom of a trend. Like in the example of GS. After missing the 9:35 entry point, I would have been looking for the next top to short it. Thinking that the run would only last a couple of minutes, I would start buying puts way too soon and wind up being short all the way up a huge run. Seeing a loss in my account, I would panic and, when the stock finally changed direction, I would wait for the break even point and get out, having lost my nerve to stay in long enough to make a profit. Since my bankroll had shrunk, I was afraid to take risks. In this game, no risk, no reward.

I knew I could figure it out. I had to let go of my strategies and start from square one. This would be especially difficult considering that I was not the only one who had invested an unbelievable amount of time in developing my methods.

## End of a Good Thing

When I was in my prime, actually making a reliable $1,000-$2,000 a day using only my trading strategies, my dad offered to create a computer program to organize them. Up to that point, I had written all of the 83 different combinations of variables on two pieces of paper and had to scan through it for every stock I was considering to trade to see if there was a match. For example, if a stock traded on the NYSE, was opening up 10%, had an opening price of $24-25, it would be a *Rule 15* in my play book.

I knew nothing about creating a computer program and Dad did not know what any of my unique terminology meant. The variables were cryptic and the rules themselves looked like hieroglyphics. My pieces of paper looked like the doodles of a mad man. As long as they resulted in profits, Dad really didn't care.

It took weeks and weeks of trying phone conversations and emailing of prototypes before a working program was born. I say *born* because I think it was just about as complicated as creating a living being! I looked at the page that contained the programming language and couldn't even begin to comprehend it. What I did understand was that, when I typed a stock symbol into the appropriate field along with the previous close price and the estimated open price, a number appeared in the box below it and that number happened to be the correct rule for that combination of variables! Plus, when I clicked on the rule number, a picture popped up of my very own strategy, hieroglyphics and all! With the ability to evaluate 60 stocks in a matter of minutes, I was able to choose better stocks to trade each day, almost guaranteeing that I would hit my $2,000-a-day goal.

Almost one year later, I had to let go of the only reassuring tool I had in trading. I was now just a chaser like every other day trader out there. My trading strategies had been squashed by an ever imposing market current. I had to find stocks that would fluctuate with the market and try to find dependable entry points throughout the morning.

My bottomless bank account had hit rock bottom. The credit card offers were no longer coming in the mail. To think I once denounced that annoying junk mail! I learned that the only way to stop credit card ads is to max out your credit limit! I didn't have enough money in my checking account to transfer to my brokerage account to bring it back up to $25,000. Thus, I would be forced to trade without margin, which meant that the balance in my account would not recycle after each trade. If my account balance was $20,000 and I bought 1000 shares of a $20 stock, that would be the only trade I could make that day.

Because options are less expensive, I was forced to go back to trading them. As I mentioned before, with options comes greater volatility. For example, if you buy $5000 worth of a stock, and it goes up one point, you may make $250. However, if you buy $5000 worth of calls for that stock, in that move you may make $1000 (this is just an example, not a formula, as there are many factors that determine the gains from an options trade).

I was determined not to get sucked into the same options trap that I fell into before. If an option was only trading 100 contracts a day, I would stay away. Not enough liquidity. If the bid and ask prices were far apart, I wouldn't go near it. I found three stocks that appeared to meet my needs; GS, AAPL, and FCX. I didn't care if they were *good* stocks, as I wouldn't be holding on to them for long. What I did like was the fact that they traded many contracts per day and the bid and ask prices were always close together. *Perfect. Let the chase begin!*

My goal was no longer to make $2,000 a day, not even $1,000. My new goal was to make SOMETHING. *Stock Market Gods, if you are listening, I need my daily gains to be in the green, not red....please.* $200 a day would be enough to pay my expenses and start to pay off my credit cards. Thankfully, the cost of living in Florida is very low. $400 a day would be ideal. That would be $8,000 a month. It would be the magic amount to get my credit cards paid off before they went from the introductory, practically nothing, rates, to the nose bleed rates. Up until that point I had been trying to recover from my losses quickly and I just wound up digging myself further and further into the money pit. No more.

Having determined that I would be living in Florida permanently, I decided to find a doctor. I knew I was healthy. Stressed, but healthy. The initial visit was quick. Blood pressure fine, heart fine, weight a little under normal but fine. All I needed to do was get my blood work done. I fasted overnight and headed over to the lab Saturday morning. Years ago I would have been in total trauma. One look at the needle and I would faint...out cold! Not anymore. I twirled my hair at an alarming rate while the blood was being drawn but managed to stay upright.

A few days later the results came in. I had the cholesterol and triglycerides of a 300-pound couch potato! It turned out that, while all that cholesterol-laden seafood didn't make me fat, it made my blood positively obese! Me, who stood on my soap box preaching healthy living to anyone who would listen. I was now on my way to an early grave!

Luckily I was an expert in dietary restriction. Overnight I went back to my tasteless vegan diet. I reprimanded servers who dared to bring me a salad with the dressing already on it, and I began my obsessive label reading again. I was determined to get my lipid panel as well as my bank account out of the red.

Until then, I was forced to *shop on a budget*. Never in my life had I ever uttered that phrase! Even in high school I had money to burn. I was an assistant teacher at the dance studio and the money I earned went directly to my clothing account. I had shopping down to a science and spent every spare minute exacting it.

It was not a matter of going to the mall to get *things I needed*, it was about making sure that everything that came in my size and fit my taste was not overlooked. The thought of missing the perfect sweater was unbearable. I could leave no display unturned. Plus, trying on clothes burns as many calories as speed walking, at least for me! I treated my shopping trips like a mini-marathon. At the end, with little beads of sweat on my forehead, I would make my way back to my car with full shopping bags (that was the strength training part of my workout), feeling very accomplished.

In Manhattan, I took these shopping trips to the next level, Madison Avenue. Sales associates had me sized up from the start. They saw me surveying the store as soon as I walked in. I was not there to sightsee, I meant business. Their job was to cater to shopping addicts and I was their whale.

Now, in Florida, I was forced to enter forbidden territory...the *outlet*. With my baseball cap and sunglasses on, I crept in. I had made my bed and now I would have to lie in it...in factory closeout pajamas! I made my choice, stocks over clothes, options contracts over shoes. I was wallowing in the bottom of the money pit.

With years of expert shopping skills under my belt, I was determined that I could make this work. I knew that I could find a few diamonds in the rough, and there was a lot of *rough*. *Rough* as far as the eye could see. Paper thin, disposable clothes with gaudy prints, grandma-style plaid pants, even elastic waistbands, for God's sake! The racks were long and the clothes were jumbled. Not a personal shopper in sight. This would take awhile. There was no question that the prices were right. I could buy ten outfits for the cost of one in New York. Four hours later, that's exactly what I did. There was not a single *diamond* left in the store. Mission accomplished. If only I had this aptitude for choosing stocks!

When I got to the counter, the cashier offered me another 15% off if I opened a store credit card. I was sure there was no way that I would be approved; I had already hit my credit limit. Deciding to risk the humility of being declined, I held my breath as she entered in my social security number and all the other information necessary to do a credit check. Seconds later, with a big smile, she handed me my temporary card with a credit limit of $1000. I had been approved! I was wondering if

**End of a Good Thing**

the nice lady would be so kind as to make a balance transfer into my brokerage account. I decided to just go back and choose some factory closeout bras.

### End of a Good Thing

## QUADRUPAL WITCHING DAY

7:00 as usual, the alarm goes off, and I have breakfast, blah, blah, blah. Today, however, will be a bit different. It is "Quadruple Witching Day." I don't know why it is called that, all I know is that for me it is "Quadruple Bitching Day." This is the day when options (as well as other things that I don't trade so therefore don't care about) expire. As I mentioned before, options contracts expire every month. The closer you get to the expiration day, the more volatile the option trading gets. Finally, on THE DAY you can see the price of a contract jump from ten cents to a dollar in a matter of minutes. For those who have an aptitude for chasing moving stocks, there is much money to be made on this crazy day. But, if you are like me, this day will drive you to drink!

9:30 I turn the volume down on the TV. I know that ^*&#$@ bell is ringing and I don't want to hear it!

9:35 I am watching my "pet" stocks, AAPL, FCX, and GS waiting for an entry point. FCX is running up now and, although 9:35 is a good time for a change of direction, I know that this stock can run in one direction for a good ten minutes so I pass. AAPL is not moving much. That makes me nervous. I'll check on that one later. GS is at a high point. I buy puts thinking it will change course.

9:40 I have made money on GS. It is down now. I sell

my puts for a profit and buy calls thinking it will start going up again.

9:45 it's still going down. I buy more calls in an attempt to "price average."

9:50 it's STILL GOING DOWN!

10:00 *all the other stocks that have been going down have turned around and are running up...NOT GS! Why didn't I go with AAPL or FCX? They are going up now!* I am in deep with a loss. It seems that the whole market has decided to be positive except for the financial sector. GS is sitting at the bottom with no upward momentum in sight.

11:30 my eyes have glazed over. It is Friday and Mom and I are going to a dog adoption event at noon. I have half an hour to decide if I'm going to hold on to my calls and gamble that the stock will go up later on today, or take my loss and forget about it.

12:00 PM I hear Mom's car in the driveway. Because it is expiration day, if I hold on to my contracts with a $140 strike price and the stock closes below $140, I am out everything, thousands of dollars. I can't take that chance. I sell my calls and call it a day.

12:30 PM we are at the dog adoption event. *Awwww, cute dogs! I would definitely trade better if I had a nice furry dog sitting next to me!*

2:00 PM I'm back at the computer. GS is UP! Had I held on to the contracts, I would have not only

### End of a Good Thing

recovered from my loss but made $1,000!

2:01 PM I have a Classic Quadruple Witching Day Hissy Fit.

4:00 PM I play a few hands of online poker to wind down. It is a Friday after a hectic week. If I stop trading/gambling too fast I may get The Bends.

# Chapter 12

# Currency: The Heroin of Day Trading

A few days later while I was cooling off at the pool, a couple whom I had met before floated over to me. I knew that he was a retired hedge fund manager and they knew I was a day trader. We had chatted about the stock market before but nothing more than casual conversation. Today he seemed to have a mission.

"How was trading today?" He asked.

I was really regretting that I had told everyone I was a trader. "A little slow today. Earnings season will start in a couple weeks so it should pick up then."

"Have you ever traded the Forex?"

"I haven't gone near it. Heard that it is too dangerous."

"Not any more dangerous than the stock market. I

would much rather trade currency. It is much more reliable than trading a company's stock. Plus, you can make tons of money really fast!"

That voice in the back of my head started screaming: *Paddle away! Paddle away!* I hadn't listened to that voice of reason once in the past three years. Why should I start now? I stayed right there in the deep end, treading water, as he sang the praises of Forex trading.

"For example, today at 8:30 when the jobless claims came out, the USD/EUR dropped 80 pips!"

"Excuse me? The *what* dropped *what*?"

"The USD/EUR is a currency pair. A pip is an increment of the price. It was a huge drop!"

He continued to explain how Forex trading works and the benefits. Just like options can bring a greater return than stocks with less funds, Forex is similar but with *even less* money you can make *even more* money. At least that's how I heard it. Since I was down to $3,000 in my brokerage account, I was all ears.

After coming off another frustrating week in the stock market, I finally saw a ray of light. We had been chatting in the pool for awhile. I had turned into a prune, but at least I was a hopeful prune. I made a hasty exit from the pool area, hopped in my golf cart, and sped home. I was ready to open a Forex account and transfer what was left of my money into it, my last opportunity to trade.

## Currency: The Heroin of Day Trading

Having experience with several stock trading platforms, I acclimated quickly to the Forex platform. As soon as I saw the currency pairs, the pips, I got it. It was money and it was moving. Enough said. I had been spending the last few weeks trying to find stocks that moved in tandem with the market but was getting murdered when company news or sector news altered the stocks' movement. I was ready to move on and trading currency appeared to be the way to go. *"Let the chase begin!"*

I opened up a little Forex trading account even though I only had $1000 left to trade with after paying my bills. The great thing about Forex trading is that you are given *leverage*. With the online broker that I chose, that leverage was 400/1 meaning that I could actually purchase much more than $1000 worth of currency. I could actually make a decent living trading with just $1000 in my account, if I didn't mess up! Since the Forex market is open twenty-four hours a day, I could trade not only when the market moved because of news in the USA but also Japan, Australia, The UK, Canada, the whole world!

I found a site on the internet that lists global economic events on a calendar. Each day I made sure I was at the computer when important information was to be released and traded around those events. I set up my platform with the charts of eight currency pairs that appeared to be most active so I could watch for any major movement.

I was reluctant to use all of my leverage on a trade. I knew if I made a mistake and lost all of my money that it would be the final nail in my coffin. I had $1000 left in my checking account, or more accurately, $1000 left in my overdraft account. My plan was to make $100 a day my first week just to gain confidence and get acclimated with currency trading. I wanted to be able to make a withdrawal by the end of the week for no other reason than to get the feel of *earning* money again.

By Friday I had managed to come out only $100 ahead but also, I believed, much wiser. I had gotten a taste of how currency moves *and* I didn't get slaughtered in the process. I made a withdrawal of $100. I was hooked. I had no doubt I would do much better the following week.

## Chapter 13

## Welcome to the Money Pit My Furry Friend!

My first week of currency trading was behind me. That weekend I was on a mission. I now had a source of income again and my maternal time clock was ticking. I wanted a baby! A furry baby! I had never wanted to *have* a baby. I had nightmares in which I was eight months pregnant, fat, and at the point of no return. I would wake up in a cold sweat but thoroughly relieved to find myself with a flat stomach. I always smile when I see mothers with screaming kids in restaurants or in stores. Not because I think they are cute, but because I am thinking *no matter how tough my life is right now, it could be worse.* No, a human baby was not in the cards for me.

I had been in pursuit of a dog for the past year. I was

tired of going to neighborhood dog parades and dog parks without a dog. Kind of felt like an adult going to a playground without a kid, creepy! I went to every dog adoption event within a hundred mile radius but had yet to find my perfect pet. I had been licked by hundreds of dog tongues and had petted so many dogs that I was starting to lose my fingerprints. Still, no luck. I was determined to adopt a dog that had been rescued, that needed a home. I refused to even consider a breeder or pet store. No way that I would support the practice of breeding dogs for profit. I just had to find my ideal dog...a mid-sized furry dog with a flat back, good for petting. Nope, no furless spiny backs for me! I didn't want to feel like I was playing a xylophone every time I stroked its back!

Every weekend I went to a local flea market where an animal rescue group brought newly found dogs. The volunteers had come to know me well. I was really hoping that one week I would find a dog that just clicked with me. Most of their dogs were large and best suited for a farm or house with a fenced-in yard. They rescued many dogs from puppy mills that had been raided and closed down. The poor mama dogs had spent their lives in small cages with barely enough room to stand up, having litter after litter of puppies. They never knew what it is like to walk on grass, or anything for that matter other than a cage floor. The puppies were

### Welcome to the Money Pit My Furry Friend!

so cute! If they stopped growing and stayed that size I would have taken one but, judging by the size of their paws, they would quickly outgrow my house.

Finally, I found a website that features rescued dogs available for adoption. You can search by location, breed, size, age, and more. I found an adorable black Pomeranian, with an adoption fee of $400. His foster mom agreed to a weekend trial at my house while she and her family went on vacation.

"One thing I should tell you. He was checked by the vet and I was told that he has bad knees. It is a condition very common to small dogs. Do you still want him?"

I did some research on the condition and learned that knee surgery is the only option for solving the problem. Cost, $2000. I called the foster mom back and apologized for not being able to take on such an obligation. She understood.

Next, two visits were scheduled with other foster families, each about an hour and a half away. The first agreed to meet in a local dog park with two of the dogs I was interested in. My mom and dad went with me. I was getting serious now. I really felt that I was close to finding my dog and wanted Grandma and Grandpa there to meet their grand puppy.

It was Sunday and the park was reasonably quiet. We sat on a bench awaiting their arrival. Finally a lady, her daughter and two pups bounced through the gate. My mom and dad agreed to stay back and let me meet the dogs alone so there would be fewer distractions. I approached them and noticed that the Yorkie only had three legs.

"Did I forget to mention that he had to have his leg amputated?" The lady asked sheepishly.

I was open to adopting a special needs dog but, after a little petting session, the chemistry just didn't feel right. The second dog was a Corgie. He seemed more interested in marking the trees than meeting me. I tried to connect with him but it didn't happen. Watching the interaction, my parents weren't surprised. They could tell that I hadn't found my dog today. I was sorry that they had to make the trip to just see 1 ¾ dogs.

Monday morning we were off again. This time to a veterinarian's office also about an hour and a half away. Three dogs being boarded there were from a Schnauzer and Wirehaired Terrier rescue group. Again, my parents sat in the waiting room while I was led into an examination room to meet the dogs one by one. The first dog was a Terrier who immediately started bouncing off the walls after he was led into the little room from his kennel. I tried to pet him, talk to him, and calm him down but he was hyper. After a quick visit he was led away.

A Miniature Schnauzer was next in line for the meet and greet. He came over to me immediately. He was 25 pounds, a bit on the pudgy side for his breed. His coat was a beautiful salt and pepper and very soft. He sniffed and sniffed with his cute licorice nose while I stroked him. His cute Schnauzer snout made him look like a little old man even though he was only three. His tail had been docked when he was a puppy so all he had was a little stump, albeit a cute stump. I had found my dog!

There was one more to meet. For me it was only a formality. He was a smaller Schnauzer, a bit on the skinny side. He started running laps around the exam room as soon as he came in. I tried to make contact with him for a quick pat on one of his trips past me but he was moving too fast.

"What do you think?" The kennel keeper asked.

"Can you bring the second dog back in? I want him to meet my mom and dad; I think he is the one!"

I called out to my parents in the waiting room and they came in and fell in love with him as quickly as I did. I just had to fill out the paperwork, pay the vet bill, and I had my new furry baby! My dad came up with his name...Winston.

Welcome to the Money Pit My Furry Friend!

## DAY TRADING WITH A DOG

6:30 the dog goes off. He at least tries to be polite about it but he makes it very clear that this is wake-up time. After a few minutes of listening to his snorting by my bed, I get up and give him a little pat on the way to the bathroom. This makes him very happy and he wags his stump and sits while I try to make myself presentable enough to go out into the dark.

6:40 with sunglasses and baseball cap on, I leash Winston and grab a page of newspaper as we head out the door.

7:00 Winston has successfully walked me around the block. I am more than happy to let him take the lead at this ungodly hour. My eyes are closed for a good part of the walk. I dispose of the poop that was neatly caught in the newspaper before it even hit the grass and proceed to the kitchen for the eagerly awaited serving of our breakfast. I feel like a Price is Right model as I open the double cabinet doors to reveal the bags of kibble and boxes of biscuits as Winston looks on, salivating.

7:05 the bowl of breakfast kibble has been devoured in record time. Wide-eyed, he awaits his turkey cube treat (with an antibiotic pill pushed into the center of it, but that's just between us).

7:10 Winston has started guard duty on the lanai while I have started trading. Every so often he will alert me if a person dares to walk past my house or a fly dares cross in front of his nose. If I'm not in a trade I will go out to acknowledge his guard work to find him looking back at me proudly while wagging his stump.

7:30 Winston decides to sleep off his breakfast under the patio table and I take a shower.

8:30 the first economic report comes out. This is the first big trading opportunity of the day. I have my hand on the mouse ready to click "buy" or "sell" depending on the market's reaction to the news. I have found that the EUR/JPY is the best currency pair to trade on news, even if it is US news.

8:35 the news is positive and the trend for the EUR/JPY is up so I continue to buy in the dips and the price rises for the next half hour.

9:15 I have made a profit but it pales in comparison to what I was making trading stocks when I was at my peak. I am just too afraid to trade enough volume to make a decent profit. I check on Winston. He is still snoring on the lanai so I continue to look for trading opportunities.

9:45 I check on Winston again. This time his ears perk up when he hears me. Yes, it is time for walk number two! It is summer in Florida so the heat is a little too much for a fast walk even at this early hour so I opt to take him to the park a couple blocks away. "Want to go for a ride in the cart????" I whisper. Within seconds he is

## Welcome to the Money Pit My Furry Friend!

on his feet, bouncing into the kitchen to find his leash, snorting the whole way. Yes, he loves riding in the golf cart!

10:15 Winston has marked every tree in the park and we are heading back home.

10:30 I am back in the computer room and Winston is watching me from the living room. He came into the computer room once while I was trading and hasn't been back since. Even the dog knows that the market is evil!

1:30 PM I am back home after getting a bite to eat for lunch and Winston greets me with a howl, which lets me know it is time for walk #3.

2:00 PM the trash can is brimming with bags of poop. I feel like my new mission in life is to pick up pooch's poop! I guess that I'm feeding him too much.

2:30 PM I drive Winston over to the vet for a weigh-in. Yep, I'm feeding him too much.

3:00 PM it's time for a quick swim in the pool before the next poop run.

4:30 PM he's pooping again.

6:00 PM Winston is drooling as I prepare his bowl of dinner kibble.

7:00 PM the overseas markets are opening so I am poised in front of the money burner waiting to pounce on the first trading opportunity. Winston is looking lonely in the living room but Mama needs to make some kibble money.

9:30 PM my eyes are glazed over. My reaction time has slowed and I am having trouble keeping track of all of the currency pairs. Time for one final walk and bed.

# Chapter 14

# Out of Money

I knew the day would finally come. Even though I was debt free when I arrived in Florida and feeling totally relieved, I knew that I was still on a slippery slope. If I didn't exercise self control, I knew I could easily lose all of my money. Back then I wasn't satisfied with making a safe $500 a day. Even though my bank account was in the black, I felt I *had* to make back the money I had lost early on and I had to do it quickly.

Exactly one year later, all I had to live off of was what little available credit I still had on my credit cards. I had lost all of my money and was deep in debt with no sign of a stable income on the horizon. A good day trading currency yielded less than $200. On a bad day, that's how much I lost. I was managing to come out a little ahead each week but I was not making enough to cover my bills.

After a few weeks of currency trading, I realized that if I didn't have a natural sense of timing when it came to trading stocks, the same would apply with currency. I had tried catching a run-up, shorting a drop, and trying to find the exact entry point before a change of direction. My trading account dwindled from $1,000 to $100. The money I was making on short term trades wasn't substantial enough to balance out the the losses when I held on to a bad trade too long. Why couldn't I have the same tenacity when I was in a good trade? Why did I only grit my teeth and hang on when I was losing money? Why did the same scenario repeat itself day after day? If I did the exact opposite I would be making $1000 a week! I just couldn't figure out how to get out of my losing mind-set.

With the mortgage payment due in a week, I went through my house to determine what I could sell to cover it. Ebay had once been a hobby and now it was my last hope to remain financially independent. I had promised myself I would tell my parents what I had gotten myself into when things became serious but I could never get up the nerve. I was their only child, their biggest investment, and I had gone Chapter 11! How do you break that kind of news?

I quickly found out that in the 2009 economy, Ebay

does not bring in the buyers that it did just a couple years prior. Luckily, I was able to sell a few high-priced items locally. I had mortgage money for at least a month. The utility bills would have to wait.

Meanwhile, I had a new responsibility...the pooch. His vet bills had been paid and I had enough kibble to last a lifetime so he was certainly not a financial burden. He was actually what helped me to keep my sanity. Long petting sessions with a warm furry dog can do wonders for lowering a speeding heart rate. Five or six high speed walks in the fresh air lifts the spirits. I was just afraid of what would happen if there was an emergency, if Winston did require expensive treatment at some point in the future.

Friday rolled around and the currency market was about to close for the weekend. I was ready to implement a new trading idea. I stumbled on it by accident the week before. I thought that the currency market closed at 5PM on Friday when trading actually stops at 4PM. I was still holding a long position when the market closed and I feared that, when trading resumed Sunday night, the price would open much lower and I would lose the rest of my money.

After a stressful weekend, I opened up my trading platform Sunday night to find that the price had indeed dropped. My position, however, had been closed out at the "stop price" that I had set up when I opened the trade. Whew! I only lost $20! How great that they honored my stop price even though the pair was trading at a much lower rate!

Seeing this new opportunity, I decided to hold a position overnight, this time intentionally. I took a gamble that the GPB/USD would open down on Sunday night when the market re-opened. I would place a "stop order" to make sure that, if I was wrong, I would only lose $50. The brokerage I was using honored stops so, if I shorted the pair at 1.6948 and entered a stop at 1.70 and it actually went as high as 1.71 at the open, I would be out at 1.70. If I was correct and the price dropped, I would make money.

Of course, I forgot that a new rule was passed banning the use of stop orders and it would take effect as soon as the market re-opened on Sunday! Do I even need to mention that the price of the pair went up? I think we all know my luck by now. I lost all the money in my account.

Now I really had to tighten the belt. Time to buy the store brand cereal and opt for the big bag of grapes in the produce section instead of the high priced berries. Pooch was also due for a grooming and so was I. A wash and cut for both of us would ring in at $100. Considering that I couldn't even afford to pay the cable bill, I decided to attempt beautifying both of us myself.

My hair was not that difficult, I just hacked away at it until it looked shorter, neater, and relatively even along the bottom. Before taking the scissors to Winston, I did some research. I pulled up a "How to Groom Your Schnauzer" instructional video on Youtube. How easy they make it look with their electric shavers and numbered scissors designed especially to cut fur! After a few failed attempts at getting His Highness to stand still, I decided to wait till he was on his back and half asleep. I slowly cut the fur that was the most accessible until I had made a nice little fur pile on the rug. He certainly did not have a show-dog cut but he was wearing less fur. Mission accomplished.

Meanwhile, I made sure that he was not exceeding his recommended amount of kibble and getting five or six fast-paced walks per day. Winston's fear of other dogs appeared incurable. The only solution was to pick him up and carry him for part of the walk if there was another dog in sight. This proved to be very calming for him but exhausting for me. He was like a 26-pound furry medicine ball!

The vet also advised against giving him milk bones as rewards. They are empty calories...Twinkies for dogs. Instead, I was giving him three-calorie treats...rice cakes for dogs. I felt bad eating in front of him so I took my meals while he was sleeping. We did have one minor setback when he discovered a goldmine on one of our walks. Eight hot dogs had been left in the bushes in the park after a picnic. He went after them like he hadn't seen food in a year! By the time I realized what he had gotten into, one or two had made it down the hatch. Despite that, I was sure that he had lost at least a couple pounds. After a month I took him back to the vet for another weigh-in. He had gained a pound! I, on the other hand, had lost five.

The bill pile was getting higher. It was killing me that I had the outlet store credit card with a $1,000 credit line available that I could only use for merchandise purchases in their store. How many pairs of elastic waistband pants could one own? Then I had a stroke of genius. If only I could find something in that pathetic place that was actually in demand. I could buy it with my store credit card and then sell it on Ebay and get the *cash* for the item. But who would pay for elastic granny pants?

While watching TV a few nights later, I actually came across a commercial that piqued my interest. It was for a new sneaker. After seeing the ad I just *had* to have that sneaker! A quick Ebay search revealed that I wasn't the only one! There were only a few pairs up for auction and they had bids. High bids! I got on the phone and, believe it or not, the outlet store had that exact sneaker in stock. I bought as many pairs as I could without going over my

## Out of Money

credit limit and immediately listed them on Ebay.

I then applied for credit cards at other stores and repeated the process. Apparently I was still credit worthy in the eyes of desperate retailers! Walmart had a nice promotion, no interest for a year on a $250 purchase made with their credit card. They didn't have the popular sneakers so I had find something else to buy there. I wanted to be practical. I loaded the cart with the highest priced essential item that I could think of...Tampons. With my luck, I thought, I'll go into early menopause!

I realized that this sneaker fad wouldn't last forever, and neither would the store credit card offers. I felt like a money scrounging vulture and I wound up where many others do in the same situation, at the Lotto counter of the local liquor store.

I had studied the odds carefully online and was ready with my strategy. My last ounce of sanity was at stake and it rested on the plexiglas cabinet of scratch off tickets and the sales lady behind the counter.

"I'll have five number fourteen tickets and five number eight tickets please."

The odds were 1:4.3 so if I got five of the same tickets, there had to be a winner in there somewhere! I raced home and, with Winston at my feet looking up at me quizzically, I began scratching. *Loser, loser, loser, $100! Loser, $20! Loser, loser, $40! Loser.* I had come out ahead!

## I Fell Into the Money Pit: Memoirs of an Unlikely Day Trader

No, I did not win the life-changing, or in my case life-saving, $250,000, but I did make some money, enough to keep trying.

After my fourth visit to the Lotto counter in one day, the staff knew me well. I am sure they were exchanging stories about the wild-eyed, half-crazed, scratch-off queen! But what did I care? I was up $165 in one day!

The next morning I ran Winston around the block, took a quick shower and headed back to my office...the Lotto counter. I only wished they had the sense to put bar stools there! Maybe even come around with some refreshments. A man was in line behind me waiting to check out with his bottle of whiskey. He quickly sized up the situation.

"Those things can be addictive, can't they?"

I was in no mood for small talk. Eying his booze, I shot back, "At least with a Lotto ticket you have a chance of winning something. All you can hope for is to be at the top of the list for a new liver!"

That shut him up.

The next day I repeated the same process. This time I was on a losing streak. I finally stopped when I was down to $100 profit. I needed that money to cover the finance charges that were about to post to my credit card. If I didn't get the funds there in time, I would lose my low introductory APR.

While I was scratching Lotto tickets, Winston was

## Out of Money

scratching himself...all night! *Scratch, scratch, scratch, lick, lick, lick, SNORT.* That final *snort* woke me up every time. He seemed to be a bit congested. Note to self, dust in the morning! After giving him a close inspection from nose to tail, I noticed he had stump trouble...little red bumps. I decided it was time to pay the vet another visit. Thankfully, I had picked up a brochure for a pet care credit card application. Otherwise, Winston's next trip to the doctor would have left me broke. Like the store credit cards, I was also approved for this. Now Winston had started digging his own money pit right next to mine.

Chapter 15

Getting Out of a Rut the Hard Way

How could it be that I was actually happier sitting in the bottom of the money pit than I was when I was sitting on the top of a pile of money? Did it take losing everything to get to the point where I actually had what I really wanted?

When I moved to New York City I thought I was on the fast track to achieving my perfect life. I wanted to dance in New York, be independent, have a job with a six-figure income, own a Manhattan apartment, be rich, and be envied. Not many from my little home town could accomplish those things and I felt that, if I did, I would be content for the rest of my life.

Back then, I couldn't imagine the day when I would not be able to find happiness in being financially well off. I didn't think that I would ever want to leave a job that afforded such a great lifestyle. I never thought the day would come when I would no longer feel a sense of excitement when a dance class started. However, after awhile, I found myself choosing to sleep in, in my nice warm apartment, rather than battle the cold city to get to ballet class on Saturday. If I wasn't driven to dance anymore, why was I still staying in the city in a job that only brought me money and no other professional satisfaction? Was I destined to become an ordinary nine-to-five working stiff who could only find enjoyment in shopping and other mundane activities?

No, it was definitely time for a change, no matter how life altering. I never did do *ordinary* and *mundane* well. I have always believed that if you find yourself saying "in my next life I will do x" (whatever it is you are hoping for), you need to start making changes in *this life.* I was finding myself saying "in my next life, I will live in a warm place with palm trees." Or, "in my next life, I will adopt a dog." Admittedly, they are simple goals, but when you are trapped in a lifestyle that appears to be too good to leave, they seem a lifetime away.

Of course I wish that I had the nerve to just sell my apartment and move to Florida *before* I gambled my money away, but I was not willing to take a step back. I did not want to take a job that paid less than what I was making in New York and there was no job in Florida that would have matched it. When I discovered the stock market, I thought I had found my salvation—a job that I could do from my laptop anywhere in the world.

I must say that I feel that I have really *lived* the last five years. Yes, thirty to thirty-five have been juicy. Looking back, I crammed a lot of excitement into my first two years in New York City, but once I began working at the employment agency, the days just blended together. As scary as my situation is now, I am more frightened to think of my life had I continued on the same path. Would I still be sitting at the same desk doing the same job sucking down one Frappachino after another?

It is clear that my life changed course after I made my first stock trade and I can only believe that it changed for a reason, and that I will eventually find out that it did indeed change for the better. Until then, I will walk my little furry baby around the park, let him pee on all the palm trees and maybe, if I'm nice to him, he will help dig me out of the money pit.

In my search to find a *furry baby* I discovered the Humane Society of Inverness in central Florida. They are devoted to the rescue of dogs that have been rescued from "puppy mills" that have been raided and shut down. As a no-kill shelter, they do what it takes to nurse them back to health and to care for them until they are well enough to be placed with a forever family. I have met many of the volunteers and can tell you that this organization truly cares about animals. Right now, they have many, many dogs and cats to care for and very limited funds. Know that whatever you are able to contribute will go directly to the care of their rescues and that your gift will be greatly appreciated!

**You can make a donation directly to the Humane Society of Inverness at www.hsinverness.com**

www.ingramcontent.com/pod-product-compliance
Lightning Source LLC
Chambersburg PA
CBHW032113090426
42743CB00007B/339